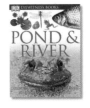

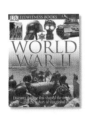

ARCTIC & ANTARCTIC

Arctic plant

Net for catching ptarmigan

Reindeer-skin winter coat from Siberia

Siberian shaman's staff

Antarctic explorer's compass

Siberian ivory model of reindeer drawing a sled

Rosebay
willow
herb

Snowshoe
for a pony

DK EYEWITNESS BOOKS

ARCTIC &
ANTARCTIC

Written by
BARBARA TAYLOR

Photographed by
GEOFF BRIGHTLING

Carving of polar
bear from Canada

Dorling Kindersley

Model of Greenland canoe

Engraved ivory

DK

Dorling Kindersley

LONDON, NEW YORK, AUCKLAND, DELHI, JOHANNESBURG, MUNICH, PARIS and SYDNEY

Cribbage board made from walrus tusk

For a full catalog, visit

DK www.dk.com

Project editor Gillian Denton
Art editor Jane Tetzlaff
Managing editor Simon Adams
Managing art editor Julia Harris
Editorial assistance Gin Von Noorden and David Pickering
Researcher Céline Carez
Production Catherine Semark
Picture research Clive Webster

This Eyewitness ® Book has been conceived by
Dorling Kindersley Limited and Editions Gallimard

© 1995 Dorling Kindersley Limited
This edition © 2000 Dorling Kindersley Limited
First American edition, 1995

Published in the United States by
Dorling Kindersley Publishing, Inc.
375 Hudson Street,
New York, NY 10014
10 9

Dorling Kindersley books are available at special discounts for bulk purchases for sales promotions or premiums. Special editions, including personalized covers, excerpts of existing guides, and corporate imprints can be created in large quantities for specific needs. For more information, contact Special Markets Dept., Dorling Kindersley Publishing, Inc.

Shaman's eagle from Siberia

Library of Congress Cataloging-in-Publication Data
Taylor, Barbara, (1954–).
Arctic & Antarctic / written by Barbara Taylor; photographed by Geoff Brightling.
p. cm. — (Eyewitness Books) Includes index.
1. Zoology — Polar regions — Juvenile literature. 2. Polar regions — Juvenile literature.
[1. Zoology — Polar regions. 2. Animals — Habits and behavior. 3. Polar regions.]
I. Brightling, Geoff, ill. II. Title. III. Title: Arctic and Antarctic.
QL104.T48 2000 508.311—dc20
ISBN 0-7894-5851-9 (pb)
ISBN 0-7894-5850-0 (hc)

Color reproduction by Colourscan, Singapore
Printed in China by Toppan Printing Co. (Shenzhen) Ltd.

Siberian shaman's apron

Both the Arctic and Antarctic support some plant life

Husky dogs

Contents

Snowy owl

The ends of the Earth

THE TWO POLAR REGIONS at the very ends of the Earth are among the coldest, windiest, and most remote places on the planet. A huge, frozen ocean – the Arctic – surrounds the North Pole; a vast area of frozen land – Antarctica – surrounds the South Pole. Both the Arctic and Antarctic have long, dark, freezing winters. During the short summer, the sun shines all the time, and animals flock to the polar areas to feed and nest. The Arctic and Antarctic are the last two wilderness areas on earth. However, the Arctic has already been exploited for its mineral wealth, and both polar regions are increasingly threatened by pollution, mining, and other human pressures.

The position of the Arctic and the Antarctic

TRAPPED BY THE ICE
In 1596, a Dutch explorer, William Barents, set off on his third attempt to find a route from Europe to China and India around the North Pole. When his ship was trapped by sea ice, he and his crew were forced to winter ashore, building a cabin from the wrecked ship. In spring, the men set off for Europe in the ship's boats. Barents himself died, but his men survived.

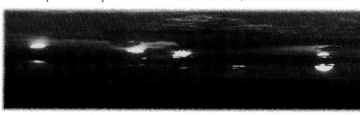

Long tongues of ice extend into the sea from the edges of ice sheets

An unstructured slush known as frazil ice forms below the surface

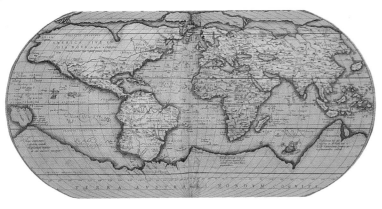

NORTHERN LIGHTS
Auroras are wispy curtains of light that appear in the sky above the poles. They can sometimes take the form of brilliantly colored shooting rays. Auroras are caused by charged particles from the sun striking gases in the earth's atmosphere above the poles. This makes the gases give off light.

MYSTERY LAND
In the 4th century B.C., the Greek philosopher Aristotle suggested the existence of a southern landmass, known as *Terra Australis Incognita* – the unknown southern continent. Mapmakers included a huge southern continent on their maps until 1773, but it was not until Captain James Cook's explorations in the mid-18th century that anyone was able to find out what was really there.

MIDNIGHT SUN
In regions near the North and South poles, the sun never sets for several months during the summer. This happens because of the tilt of the Earth toward the sun. While one pole has constant daylight, the other is shrouded in winter darkness because the sun never rises.

In quiet waters ice often begins as thin plates, known as grease ice because they coat the water with an oily sheen

Freezing builds the ice into thicker layers; wind and waves work to break it up

The Arctic and tundra

AT THE CENTER OF THE ARCTIC REGION is a vast area of permanently frozen ice floating on the Arctic Ocean. The Arctic region also includes the largest island in the world, Greenland, the island of Spitsbergen, and the northern edges of North America, Asia, and Europe. South of the Arctic Ocean is the tundra, which means "treeless plain" in Russian. The landscape is low and flat, with many lichens, mosses, grasses, and sprawling, low bushes. Trees cannot grow in the true Arctic because they are unable to stand up to the intense cold and fierce winter winds. Water from the warmer Pacific and Atlantic oceans sometimes flows into the Arctic Ocean, warming the sea and air and clearing ice from the coasts in summer.

Marshy pools form because permafrost prevents water from draining away

MAPPING THE COAST
In 1819–1822 Sir John Franklin, who later lost his life searching for the elusive Northwest Passage (pp. 52–53), made a hazardous land expedition charting the coast of Canada. At one point he took to canoe, which was particularly dangerous as the ice was breaking up. Wooden ships and boats of the 19th century could easily be crushed or trapped by ice.

The "tree line" where forest gives way to tundra is often taken to be the southern boundary of the true Arctic

Frozen layer, called permafrost, a little way below the surface; it never thaws out

BEAR JOURNEYS
Polar bears live only in the Arctic. They make long journeys across the Arctic pack ice, hunting for seals. The bears are expert divers and swimmers, and often hitch rides on ice floes. One polar bear was found swimming 200 miles (320 km) from land. Polar bears can also dive from the top of icebergs more than 50 ft (15 m) into the water.

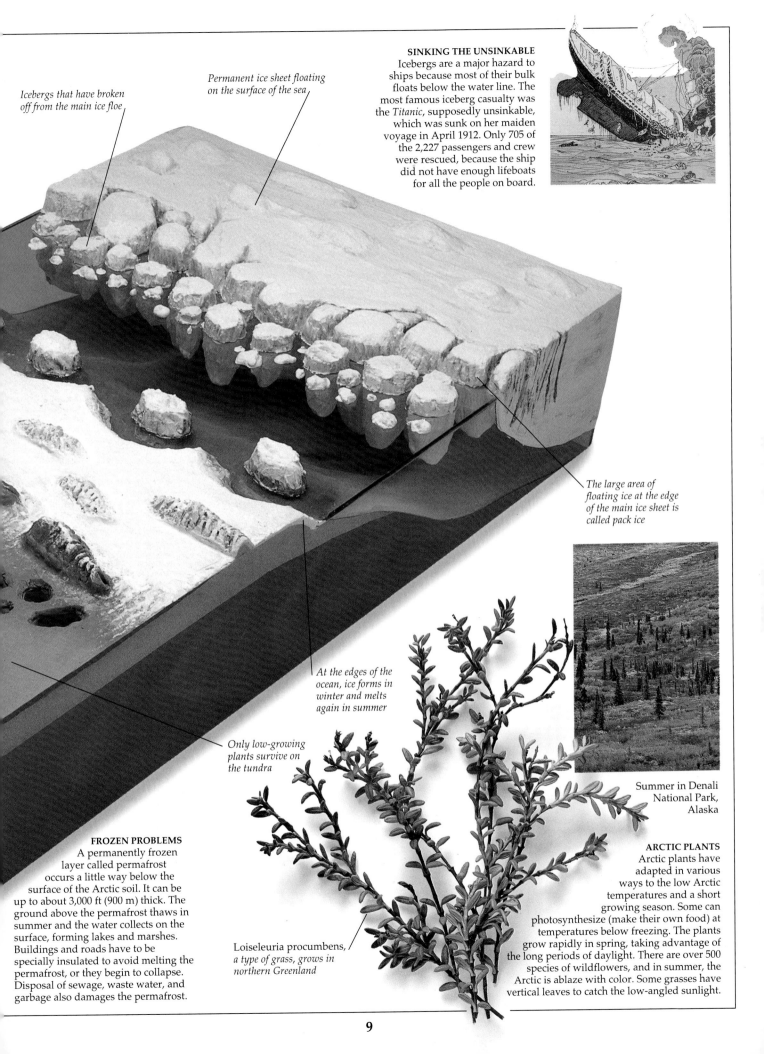

Icebergs that have broken off from the main ice floe

Permanent ice sheet floating on the surface of the sea

SINKING THE UNSINKABLE
Icebergs are a major hazard to ships because most of their bulk floats below the water line. The most famous iceberg casualty was the *Titanic*, supposedly unsinkable, which was sunk on her maiden voyage in April 1912. Only 705 of the 2,227 passengers and crew were rescued, because the ship did not have enough lifeboats for all the people on board.

The large area of floating ice at the edge of the main ice sheet is called pack ice

At the edges of the ocean, ice forms in winter and melts again in summer

Only low-growing plants survive on the tundra

Summer in Denali National Park, Alaska

FROZEN PROBLEMS
A permanently frozen layer called permafrost occurs a little way below the surface of the Arctic soil. It can be up to about 3,000 ft (900 m) thick. The ground above the permafrost thaws in summer and the water collects on the surface, forming lakes and marshes. Buildings and roads have to be specially insulated to avoid melting the permafrost, or they begin to collapse. Disposal of sewage, waste water, and garbage also damages the permafrost.

Loiseleuria procumbens, a type of grass, grows in northern Greenland

ARCTIC PLANTS
Arctic plants have adapted in various ways to the low Arctic temperatures and a short growing season. Some can photosynthesize (make their own food) at temperatures below freezing. The plants grow rapidly in spring, taking advantage of the long periods of daylight. There are over 500 species of wildflowers, and in summer, the Arctic is ablaze with color. Some grasses have vertical leaves to catch the low-angled sunlight.

The Antarctic

THE CONTINENT OF ANTARCTICA is twice the size of Australia, and one and a half times the size of the United States. It is also three times higher than any other continent; almost all of it is covered by an ice sheet that is, on average, 8,000 ft (2,500 m) thick. This is one major reason for the extreme cold in Antarctica. The average winter temperature is -76°F (-60°C). Antarctica's harsh climate and its isolation from other continents have greatly reduced the variety of its wildlife – the largest animal that lives on land all year round is a tiny insect. During the summer, however, many animals, including penguins, whales, and seals, visit the continent to take advantage of the rich food supply and safe breeding sites around the coasts. Plants are very sparse, and consist mostly of lichens, mosses, and liverworts.

SOLE SURVIVOR
Mosses are one of the few plants able to survive in Antarctica. There are about 80 species of these tough little plants in the region. They grow in dense mats and cushions for protection from the weather. Dead moss builds up and forms banks of peat that can be several feet thick.

WARMER CLIMATE
Antarctica was not always cold. Fossil ferns (above) provide evidence of a warmer, subtropical climate about 70 million years ago. Over hundreds of millions of years, the land that is now Antarctica probably drifted to the bottom of the globe from near the equator.

SOUTH POLE PENGUINS
Penguins live only in the southern hemisphere. In the Arctic, auks have a similar lifestyle to penguins. They also look like penguins, but auks can fly, and penguins cannot.

Only 10 percent of an iceberg is visible above water level

ICEBERGS
When snow falls on the polar plateau, it turns into ice. The ice is compacted, and flows down toward the coastal ice shelves, where it is broken up by ocean tides, currents, and waves. This is how icebergs form. Some icebergs are so large – up to 150 miles (240 km) long and 70 miles (110 km) wide – that they can be tracked by satellites for several years before they melt.

COILED CLUES
Swimming shellfish with coiled shells, called ammonites, were common in the warm seas of prehistoric times. The last ammonites died out about 65 million years ago, but fossil ammonites found on Antarctica show that Antarctic seas were warmer millions of years ago.

WEIGHT OF ICE
About 98 percent of Antarctica is covered by an immense ice sheet, which in some places is over 2.5 miles (4 km) thick. Most of the mountains, and all of the lower ground, are buried under ice. Only a few jagged peaks, called nunataks, stick out. The enormous weight of the ice pushes most of the rocky surface of Antarctica below sea level. The ice in the lowest layers of the ice sheet is thought to be at least 200,000 years old.

DRY VALLEYS
Hidden among the Transantarctic Mountains are vast dry valleys, which are bare of snow and ice for much of the year. The valleys originally dried out because the mountains held back the ice cap. Winds rushing down the valleys suck away any moisture, forming large areas of bare rock in the middle of the continent.

CLEARING THE ICE
Special ships called ice-breakers are used to keep trade routes clear of ice during the winter. Before icebreakers, many early polar explorers saw their fragile wooden ships crushed by the power of the ice. Icebreakers have a specially shaped bow and a reinforced hull. They push the bow on top of the ice until the weight of the ship breaks through it.

Icebergs often look blue, possibly a reflection from the water

Life in Antarctic waters

In contrast to the small variety of animals on the land, there is an incredible wealth of life in the sea around Antarctica. In shallow waters, ice scrapes against the seabed, preventing any life. But in deeper waters below the crust of ice, there is a greater variety of life in the Antarctic Ocean than in the Arctic Ocean. Corals and anemones are anchored to the seabed, along with some 300 varieties of sponges. Many sea creatures feed on each other or on plankton. Food is scarce for most of the year. The cold affects the life cycles of many inhabitants. Animals function more slowly. They produce fewer, larger eggs, and care for them longer. Many animals live longer than their counterparts in warmer waters. Some sponges live for several centuries.

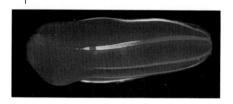

COMMON CREATURES
Antarctic squid (top) have no shell, which may be useful in icy waters, where shells grow very slowly. They seize prey in their two long tentacles. The jellyfish (bottom), which is between 0.2 in and 20 in (0.5 and 50 cm) long, is very common in Antarctic waters.

DUAL PURPOSE SPINES
Seabed animals such as the sea urchin (*Sterechinus neumayer*) may move to shallower water during the summer, when they are not in danger from ice scouring the rocks on which they live. Their dense covering of mobile spines is used for both movement and defense.

The spines of sea urchins are often poisonous

Point at the end of the leg to dig for food in the seabed

SEA LEGS
Orange sea spiders with 10 to 12 giant legs are found in deeper Antarctic waters. The pycnogonid spider (*Decolopoda australis*) has a diameter of 6 in (15 cm). It feeds on sea anemones, and like other Antarctic sea creatures, it develops very slowly.

COLD GIANTS
Many of the Antarctic's bottom-living invertebrates (creatures without backbones) are giants, such as this giant isopod *Glyptonotus antarcticus*, a relative of the woodlouse. It fills the ecological niche occupied by crabs in other parts of the world. *Glyptonotus* grows up to 8 in (20 cm), about three times bigger than similar species elsewhere. Growth is slow in the cold waters. Slow-growing invertebrates reach larger sizes than faster-growing ones. *Glyptonotus* scavenges around the seabed and eats anything it can find.

As well as the main legs, the spider has several small ones

Tentacles of coral filter out small zooplankton drifting past

ON THE ROCKS
A rock face about 26–33 ft (8–10 m) below the surface of the water provides a good anchorage for sponges, bryozoans (sea mosses), and the long hanging stalks of the soft coral *Ascolepis*. Sponges and some corals are abundant at depths of up to 0.6 miles (1 km).

Tentacles contain stinging cells that paralyze prey

TERRIBLE TENTACLES
Sea anemones capture prey, such as small fish or starfish, in their tentacles. The tentacles then pass the prey into the central "mouth" opening, ready to be digested and absorbed into the body. Waste is also excreted through the "mouth."

STAR TURN
The seabed around Antarctica is sometimes covered with colorful red starfish. Starfish locate their prey by smell, and grasp it with rows of tube feet on the underside of their legs. Antarctic starfish live long lives – one is known to have lived to the age of 39.

Tube feet for walking, digging, and grasping prey

Migrants and residents

THE NUMBER AND VARIETY of animals living near the poles changes dramatically with the seasons. Thousands of birds and mammals visit the Arctic or Antarctic only during the brief, light summer months, when it is warm and there is plenty of food available. In addition to the food supply, advantages for summer migrants include safe places to rear their young, few predators, and a lack of competition for food and nesting spots. Often, the same traditional migration routes are used each year, but the animals also navigate using the positions of the sun, moon, and stars, the earth's magnetic field, and familiar landmarks. Journeys are often very dangerous, and many animals are killed before reaching their destination by bad weather, lack of food, and predators. Only a few hardy animals, such as the musk ox, manage to stay in polar regions all year round.

Dense down feathers help to keep the geese warm

The birds save energy by flying in a V-formation in the slipstream of the one in front

Arctic tern
Sterna paradisaea

Thick skull and solid horny band protect the brain when males clash horns

Powerful wings allow the tern to cover up to 25,000 miles (40,000 km) on each round trip

Musk ox
Ovibos moschatus

CHAMPION TRAVELER
The graceful Arctic tern may see more daylight each year than any other creature. It breeds in large colonies during the Arctic summer. Then it flies all the way to the Antarctic to take advantage of the almost constant daylight and rich food supply of the Antarctic summer.

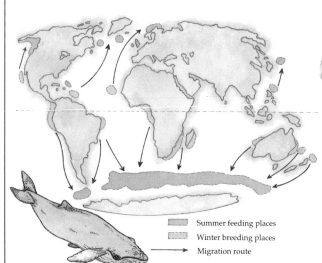

Summer feeding places
Winter breeding places
→ Migration route

Very long outer fur retains body warmth and keeps animal dry

FOOD IN THE FREEZER
Whales in both the Northern and the Southern hemispheres travel to cold polar waters in summer to take advantage of the rich food supply of plankton and fish. In winter, when the sea freezes over, they migrate back to warmer tropical waters again to breed. They eat little during their tropical stopover, relying on their immense supply of body fat, built up during the summer.

MIGHTY MUSK OX
Tough, hardy musk oxen roam over the harsh tundra in herds made up of females and young, led by one or more strong bulls. In summer, herds number about ten animals, but in winter, musk oxen move south, in herds of 50 or more, wherever they can find food under the snow. Their name comes from the smell given off by the males during the breeding season.

The male's antlers are larger and thicker than those of the females

Caribou
Rangifer tarandus

FLIGHT OF THE SNOW GEESE
Many thousands of pairs of snow geese nest in the Arctic tundra in the summer. They migrate all the way from the Gulf of Mexico, a journey of about 2,000 miles (3,200 km). On their journey, they fly in flocks of tens of thousands of birds. The shorter days at the end of summer tell the snow geese it is time to fly south once more.

Feet are tucked back during flight to make a more streamlined shape

Snow goose
Anser caerulescens

SUMMER HOLIDAYS
Caribou herds are always on the move, wandering between their winter and summer feeding grounds and snatching bites of food wherever they can find it. In spring, immense herds trek northward to feed on lichens and other low-growing tundra plants. They use well-marked trails that are often centuries old. As winter closes in, the caribou move south once more to the shelter of the forests.

Curved horns for defense against enemies such as wolves

Dense woolly underfur and thick layers of fat under the skin keep the musk ox warm

Females are smaller than males

Short, very strong legs support the massive body

Edges of hooves are sharp enough to dig through thick snow or ice to reach mosses, lichens, and roots underneath

Adaptable animals

To survive the contrasting seasons, animals have to change. As winter approaches, some mammals' fur coats grow thick. Winter fur is often white, which helps to camouflage the animal against snow. A thick layer of fat in their skin traps extra warmth and acts as a food store in lean times. Birds also have layers of fat and dense, fluffy feathers to keep out the cold. For many birds and mammals, the severe winter weather is just too much to cope with. They migrate south to warmer places, returning again in spring. Insects lay their eggs in the warmer soil, and the larvae are able to withstand the freezing temperatures of winter. As summer arrives, birds and mammals shed their thick coats. Animals that turn white in winter often have brown summer camouflage.

FINE FURS
People in cold countries wear fur clothes to keep warm through the coldest winters. They usually obtain them by snaring their original owners in traps.

Arctic fox
Alopex lagopus

DRESSED FOR SUMMER
In summer, the Arctic fox grows a thinner coat of brownish gray fur over most of its body. These colors match the brownish gray rocks of the tundra landscape, making the fox hard to see so that it can creep up on its prey, such as lemmings, without being spotted. The fox stores food under rocks during the summer and comes back to eat it in the winter months when food is hard to find. Arctic foxes have a varied diet – they eat anything from berries, shells, and dead animals to garbage and birds and their eggs.

The chest and belly are usually a pale grayish white

Short legs (and tail) lose less heat than long ones as there is less surface area exposed to the air

Thick, bushy tail can be curled around the body for warmth during blizzards or when resting or sleeping

Antarctic ice fish
Chaenocephalus aceratus

ANTIFREEZE IN ITS VEINS
Many Antarctic fishes have "antifreeze" molecules in their bodies that enable them to live in a "supercooled" state; their body fluids remain liquid at temperatures below the point at which ice forms. Antarctic ice fish (such as the fish on the left) have almost translucent (see-through) blood.

Hair under paws keeps fox from sinking in snow; the fox's Latin name is Alopex lagopus. Lagopus means "hairy foot"

Sharp claws to dig through the snow to find food

A BIRD FOR ALL SEASONS
A ptarmigan's plumage changes twice a year so that it is well camouflaged at all times. Also, the density of its feathers increases in winter. When resting overnight, ptarmigans sometimes burrow in snow to reduce heat loss.

Rock ptarmigan
Lagopus mutus

Ears are furry inside and out for extra warmth

Dense fur coat with long hairs traps body warmth

FINE TO BE FAT
Whales and seals are kept warm by a layer of thick fat called blubber. This fat walrus is in no danger of getting cold. Walruses can weigh up to 1.8 tons (1,600 kg), with tusks 3 ft (1 m) long.

Small round ears and a short muzzle cut down on heat loss; foxes from warmer places have larger ears and a longer muzzle

Sharp, pointed teeth to grab animals such as lemmings

DOUBLE-GLAZED FUR
The Arctic fox's white winter fur is made up of hairs that are hollow inside, full of air. The air in the hairs traps body warmth from the fox in much the same way as a double-glazed window traps warmth from houses. Air is a good insulator and does not let heat escape easily. The Arctic fox can tolerate temperatures of -40°F (-40°C), or even lower, quite comfortably.

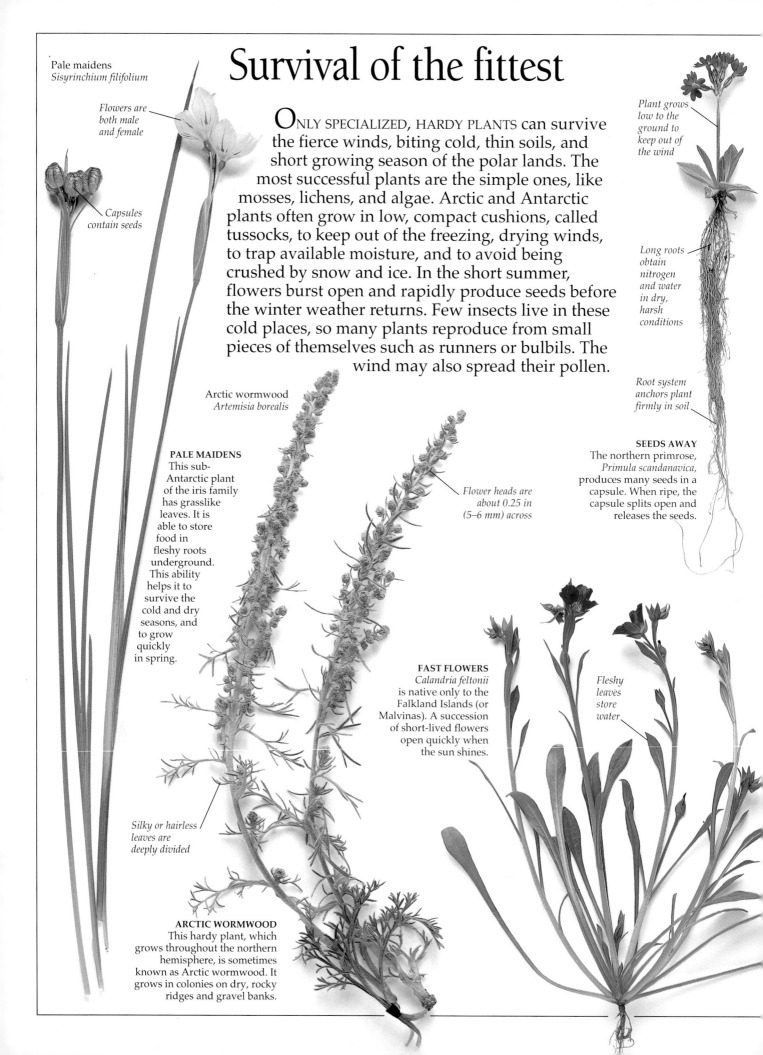

Survival of the fittest

Pale maidens
Sisyrinchium filifolium

Flowers are both male and female

Capsules contain seeds

ONLY SPECIALIZED, HARDY PLANTS can survive the fierce winds, biting cold, thin soils, and short growing season of the polar lands. The most successful plants are the simple ones, like mosses, lichens, and algae. Arctic and Antarctic plants often grow in low, compact cushions, called tussocks, to keep out of the freezing, drying winds, to trap available moisture, and to avoid being crushed by snow and ice. In the short summer, flowers burst open and rapidly produce seeds before the winter weather returns. Few insects live in these cold places, so many plants reproduce from small pieces of themselves such as runners or bulbils. The wind may also spread their pollen.

Plant grows low to the ground to keep out of the wind

Long roots obtain nitrogen and water in dry, harsh conditions

Root system anchors plant firmly in soil

SEEDS AWAY
The northern primrose, *Primula scandanavica*, produces many seeds in a capsule. When ripe, the capsule splits open and releases the seeds.

Arctic wormwood
Artemisia borealis

PALE MAIDENS
This sub-Antarctic plant of the iris family has grasslike leaves. It is able to store food in fleshy roots underground. This ability helps it to survive the cold and dry seasons, and to grow quickly in spring.

Flower heads are about 0.25 in (5–6 mm) across

FAST FLOWERS
Calandria feltonii is native only to the Falkland Islands (or Malvinas). A succession of short-lived flowers open quickly when the sun shines.

Fleshy leaves store water

Silky or hairless leaves are deeply divided

ARCTIC WORMWOOD
This hardy plant, which grows throughout the northern hemisphere, is sometimes known as Arctic wormwood. It grows in colonies on dry, rocky ridges and gravel banks.

Woolly bear
caterpillar
Arctia caja

Northern fleabane
Erigeron borealis

INSECTS OF THE NORTH
Several species of butterflies and
moths live in the Arctic regions.
The hairs of dark fuzzy
caterpillars accelerate warming
and reduce heat loss.

*Branched
flower head
is called a
panicle*

*Side branches
have spikelets
on stalks*

*Daisylike
flowers made
up of small
flowers
called florets*

Slipperwort
Calceolaria fothergillii

*Large lower
petals look
like a slipper*

INSECT REPELLENT
Low cushions of northern fleabane bloom
in the Arctic summer, when the tundra
becomes waterlogged and water collects on its
surface. The plant is highly unattractive to fleas
and midges, hence its name, and it is used
successfully by humans as an insect repellent.

*Flower sticks
out from leaves
so insects can
spot the flower
easily*

GROWTH OF GRASS
The most successful
plants in the cold polar
regions are the low-
lying mosses and
lichens. However,
several grasses
thrive in the Arctic,
like *Deschampsia
cespitosa*. On the
Antarctic mainland
only one grass
survives, *Deschampsia
flexuosa*, or Antarctic
wavy-hair grass.

*Hairy leaves
trap warmth
and moisture*

SLIPPERWORT
The rare and beautiful slipperwort grows
along the coasts of the Falkland Islands.
The color of the large, slipper-like lower
petal attracts insects, which helps the plant
to reproduce. When an insect feeds on the
plant's nectar, pollen sticks to its legs and
is carried to another slipper-flower.

TREELESS TUNDRA
The tundra, a vast zone lying between the
ice cap and the timber line of Europe, Asia,
and North America, is the habitat for many
species of plants. The harsh climate and severe
winds dictate that low-lying plants predominate
and there are no trees. To take advantage of the
short summer, some plants complete their
whole life cycle in as little time as possible.

Birds of the Arctic

FEW BIRDS CAN SURVIVE the hostile Arctic climate all year round, but residents include the ptarmigan, raven, ivory gull, and dovekie. The plumage of Arctic birds is more dense than that of migratory species, especially in the winter. Their feet are protected by feathers and do not freeze to the ice. Most Arctic birds, such as waders, shorebirds, ducks, geese, swans, and gulls, are migratory. Some migrants, particularly waders, travel long journeys in winter, as far as South America, South Africa, and Australasia. In summer, Arctic birds take advantage of the rich insect and small-mammal life on the tundra, nesting and rapidly rearing young before the winter sets in. Many different types of birds can feed and nest in close proximity because they share the available food – for instance, ducks eat water plants, seabirds eat fish, and waders eat insects.

LIKE A BIRD
In 1926, the airship *Norge* carried Norwegian Roald Amundsen and Italian Umberto Nobile over the North Pole.

HAPPY FAMILIES
The dovekie (*Alle alle*) is not much bigger than a thrush, but there are a lot of them! Over 100 million dovekies, or little auks, breed along Arctic coasts each summer. In winter, they move south but usually stay near the Arctic Circle. Dovekies have a thick layer of fat under their skin to keep them warm. They feed on the rich supply of plankton in the sea, storing food in a throat pouch.

Straight, powerful beak for stabbing prey

Long neck to probe in water beds

ON DISPLAY
Cranes mate for life. They perform spectacular courtship dances – head-bobbing, bowing, skipping, and sometimes leaping as high as 20 ft (6 m) in the air.

Streamlined, torpedo-shaped body for swimming fast underwater

REDHEADS
Sandhill cranes (*Grus canadensis*) breed mostly in the remote Arctic, laying their eggs in mounds of grass or other plants in an undisturbed marsh. Young birds stay with their parents for nearly a year. The sandhill crane's plumage often appears rusty because of reddish iron oxide stains from the water of tundra ponds. The birds probe with their bills in the mud for worms, water creatures, and frogs, then transfer the stain to their feathers when preening.

A BIRD IN THE NET
Arctic birds were an invaluable source of food for Inuit people. Hunters often caught the birds in nets on long poles.

Moving the two sticks back and forth causes the birds to bob down for their food

TOY TIME
Carving is an ancient Inuit art that often shows Arctic birds and mammals. The villages of Holman Island and Cape Dorset in Canada have become well-known for their style of art. To make this bird-feeding toy work, the two sticks are moved back and forth.

Powerful, slender, dagger-shaped beak to snap up fish and crustaceans

FEATHER BEDS
Eider ducks (*Somateria mollissima*) in the Arctic are migratory, whereas in warmer places they stay near their breeding grounds all year. Eider ducks feed mainly on shellfish, which they swallow whole. Muscles in the bird's stomach crush the shellfish. Eider ducks have particularly soft and dense down feathers for warmth. Female eiders pluck some of their breast feathers to line their nests. People use these feathers to fill quilts.

LOONY BIRDS
Loons, such as this black-throated Arctic loon, are sometimes called divers. Loons are adapted to swimming underwater after their prey, but are clumsy on land because their legs are set so far back on the body. The name loon may come from the Icelandic word *lomr*, meaning lame or clumsy. The Arctic loon breeds on tundra lakes and migrates mainly to the Pacific coast in winter.

Handsome breeding plumage; winter plumage is dull and grayish

WATER LOVERS
Loons spend most of their lives on the water and come on land only to nest. Puffins, too, are excellent swimmers and divers, hunting for shellfish in rocky coastal waters. They are ungainly on land but are able to jump from rock to rock.

Birds of the Antarctic

THE MOST COMMON Antarctic birds are seabirds, such as penguins, albatrosses, and petrels, which come ashore in summer to breed in remote, predator-free locations. They take advantage of the seas around Antarctica, which are packed with food for hungry chicks. Only 13 species of flying birds make use of ice-free land for nesting on the Antarctic mainland. The rest squash into colonies on cramped sub-Antarctic islands. Antarctic birds rely on their dense feathers and frostbite-resistant feet to keep warm, while fat reserves in the skin act as both food and insulation. Most Antarctic birds leave during the cold winter months. But some, including emperor penguins, king penguins, and wandering albatrosses, stay behind to complete their long breeding cycle. Others, such as sheathbills, only just manage to survive in the freezing winter conditions.

ANTARCTIC SCAVENGERS
Giant petrels are nicknamed "stinkers" because of their unpleasant smell. They use their powerful hooked beaks for feeding and scavenging, as well as for killing other birds. Petrels will eat almost anything, including dead seals and whales. A petrel is about the size of a vulture, with a wingspan of nearly 6.5 ft (2 m).

Wings are held up like a Viking helmet, making the bird appear large and fierce

Earsplitting shriek warns enemies to keep away

Powerful hooked beak to stab and kill prey

Antarctic skua
Catharacta maccormicki

Wings are spread to display white patches

PIRATES OF THE SKIES
Peculiar doglike barking calls signal the arrival of a pair of skuas. Skuas earn their reputation as "pirates of the skies" by chasing other birds and forcing them to regurgitate (bring up) their food. These large aggressive birds are also notorious for stealing the eggs and young of other birds. Two skuas may even cooperate while hunting, using clever tricks to snatch a meal more easily.

Brown skua
Catharacta lonnbergi

NOT FUSSY

Sheathbills are the only land birds that live year-round in Antarctica. Their success is due to their varied diet, which includes penguin and seal feces, penguin eggs, chicks, dead fish, krill, and limpets. Sheathbills also steal food intended for penguin chicks.

Horny sheath protects nostrils

Orange growths at base of beak become brighter during breeding season

Jagged, hooked bill helps to grip slippery fish

Blue-eyed cormorant
Phalacrocorax atriceps

Wings are spread out to dry off after a swim

Feathers soak up water and allow the cormorant to dive more easily

Tern

Albatross

Shearwater

Cormorant

Penguin

DIFFERENT STROKES

The pursuit of a fishy meal involves a different technique for every type of bird. Cormorants use their strong feet to paddle deep underwater after prey; penguins dive deep, then propel themselves through the sea using their wings. A tern picks fish by plunging down just under the surface of the water, and albatrosses float on the surface, keeping a sharp eye out for any possible food. Shearwaters spot their prey from the air and then plunge in pursuit.

SEAWEED NEST

Blue-eyed cormorants nest in smelly, noisy colonies close to the sea, building untidy nests of seaweed, lichens, mosses, and feathers glued together with guano (bird excrement). Blue-eyed cormorants breed on the Antarctic peninsula and on a number of Antarctic and sub-Antarctic islands. Some use their nesting sites all year round, roosting there throughout the winter. This allows them to stay near their fishing grounds in open water.

Lords of the skies

Snowy owl
Nyctea scandiaca

GHOSTLY HUNTER
Snowy owls feed primarily on the millions of lemmings living on the Arctic tundra. Owl population usually follows the rise and fall of the lemming population on its three- to four-year cycle (pp. 36–37). Many of these owls wander far south in winter.

Soapstone and ivory owl carved by Inuit craftsman in Cape Dorset, Canada

THE HUGE SUMMER BREEDING COLONIES of birds in both the Arctic and the Antarctic attract a number of predatory birds quick to enjoy the easy meals of eggs and chicks. In the Arctic, the small mammals of the tundra lands, such as lemmings and hares, increase the range of food for birds to hunt. The variety of predatory birds is therefore greater in the Arctic than in the Antarctic, and includes eagles, skuas, owls, falcons, and buzzards. The predators time their own breeding cycle to coincide with that of their prey, to ensure that their chicks will always have plenty to eat.

Feathers at tips of wings spread out like fingers to help the eagle push and steer through the air

Spread feathers help the bird to reduce speed

Strong legs to cushion impact of landing

The golden eagle slows in midair and spreads out its wings and tail to act as a brake

Eyes focused firmly on its destination, the eagle further brakes its flight by swinging out its lower body and legs

Lethal curved talons grip, crush, and carry off prey

At the last moment, its feet swing down to grip the perch

WATCH OUT BELOW
Golden eagles fly at low altitudes while hunting, then swoop suddenly to pounce on their prey. This swoop-and-grab attack is effective because it happens so swiftly that the prey is often taken by surprise. Here, a golden eagle is landing on a branch in much the same way as it would when diving for a meal.

KING OF THE CLOUDS
As the most powerful and majestic bird in the sky, the eagle features in countless stories, myths, and legends. In this illustration by British artist Reginald Knowles, a magnificent eagle perches in a tree. It appears on the title page of a collection of Norse legends.

Golden eagle
Aquila chrysaetos

Keen eyesight to spot birds and animals moving on the ground below

Powerful hooked bill to tear flesh from prey

Huge chest muscles drive the enormous wings

Feathers down to toes to keep warm

Gyrfalcon
Falco rusticolus

A KILLING MACHINE
A magnificent flier, the golden eagle is a fierce predator of ptarmigan and other birds, as well as small mammals such as ground squirrels and hares. Golden eagles usually kill their prey before carrying it off in their strong talons. They sometimes hunt in pairs, especially in winter.

FALCON FOOD
The rock ptarmigan (*Lagopus mutus*) is the gyrfalcon's main prey.

BIGGEST AND BEST
The gyrfalcon, most powerful of the falcons, relies on power and speed to catch its victims. They usually kill their prey in flight.

Ocean wanderer

THE HUGE, GENTLE ALBATROSSES of the Antarctic seas come ashore only to breed. They do not breed on the Antarctic land mass itself but on islands such as South Georgia, just north of the pack ice. There are six species of albatross that breed in the Antarctic: the black-browed, gray-headed, yellow-nosed, wandering, sooty, and light-mantled sooty. Probably about 750,000 pairs of birds breed each year. The main advantage of these isolated locations is safety from predators. Albatrosses raise only one chick at a time. The chick takes a long time to mature, sometimes remaining in the nest for up to a year. Chicks are protected from the intense cold by thick down feathers and an insulating layer of blubber, or fat. When winter begins, most albatrosses set off over the southern oceans once more.

DEAD WEIGHT
Sailors believed albatrosses brought them good luck. In Coleridge's *The Rime of the Ancient Mariner*, the unlucky mariner is forced to wear an albatross he has killed.

Black-browed albatross
Diomedea melanophris

BUMPY LANDING
Landing is a difficult task for a bird so well adapted to flying over the sea. When albatrosses approach the nest site, they circle around several times before putting their legs down, like the landing gear on an aircraft. But they often land with a bump.

Webbed feet held wide to push against the air and act as brakes

Gray-headed albatross
Diomedea chrysostoma

Large eyes indicate sharp eyesight necessary for spotting food in the sea

BIRD MAN
People have always wanted to fly like birds, but this design for an early flying machine was no challenge to the albatross's mastery of the air. For birds, like airplanes, takeoff and landing are the most dangerous parts of flying. Because of their enormous wingspan and body weight, albatrosses also need a runway to gather enough speed for takeoff.

Tube-shaped nostrils have glands at the base that excrete excess salt

Bill has razor-sharp edges to catch fish and squid

LIVING THE HIGH LIFE
Although gray-headed albatrosses weigh only half as much as wandering albatrosses, they still find it hard to take off, so they live on steep cliff sides and get extra lift from the strong winds rising up over the cliffs. Because of the harsh conditions, only half their chicks survive, a rate which is not unusually low for Antarctic birds.

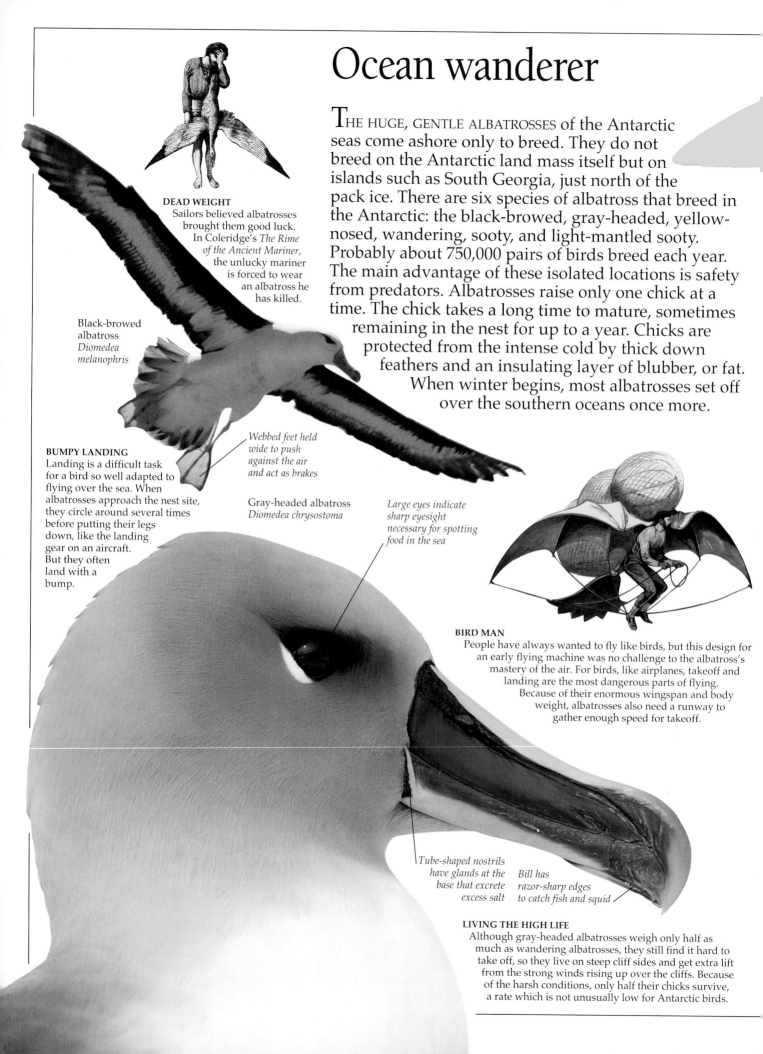

During courtship the bird points its beak to the sky and moos like a cow

FAITHFUL FLYING ACE

The wandering albatross has the greatest wingspan of any living bird. Its wing power enables the bird to cover over 300 miles (500 km) a day, alighting on the sea to feed in calm weather. Like all albatrosses, it comes ashore only to breed. The breeding cycle is exceptionally long, taking a year to complete. It therefore breeds only every two years. Breeding is preceded by an elaborate courtship display, in which the two birds dance face to face, making a variety of sounds and clapping their beaks together loudly. Wandering albatrosses usually pair for life. The most elaborate displays take place among newly formed pairs; old established partners are more discreet.

Wingspan may be between 8 ft 4 in–11 ft 10 in (254–360 cm)

SECONDHAND FOOD

Parent albatrosses feed their young by regurgitating (bringing up) the food they eat, in the form of a sticky, oily mixture. This feeding takes place when they return to the nest after many hours, or even days, of fishing out at sea. Both adults and young can use this smelly and sticky oil for defense, ejecting it with reasonable accuracy over a six-foot (2 m) range. Predators, such as skuas, may be repelled by the foul smell or immobilized if the sticky oil saturates their feathers.

Mother feeds regurgitated krill to chick

Nest is lined with grass and feathers

Nest is about 12 in (30 cm) high

BARREL NEST

The black-browed albatross makes a raised nest of mud and straw among the tussock grass.

Wandering albatross
Diomedea exulans

Strong legs and wide feet assist landing and swimming

South Pole penguins

ONE OF THE MOST SPECTACULAR SIGHTS of the Antarctic is the millions of penguins gathered at their noisy summer breeding colonies. Only two species, the Adélie and the emperor, breed on the Antarctic continent itself, but the gentoo, macaroni, chinstrap, rockhopper, and king penguins all breed within Antarctic waters. Emperor and king penguins lay a single egg each year; the other species usually lay two eggs. Penguins are supremely well adapted for swimming in cold seas. Some of these adaptations, particularly the dense, waterproof feathers and thick fat layers under the skin, also serve them well on land. The penguins rely on the fat as an energy supply when they are caring for eggs and chicks and cannot get out to sea to obtain food for themselves.

Short beak has feathers along part of its length for extra warmth

SAFETY IN NUMBERS
Penguins breed in huge, densely packed colonies called rookeries. Some rookeries contain millions of birds.

A PRACTICAL PENGUIN
Adélies winter out at sea off the pack ice but march inland to their breeding colonies in October. They navigate partly by means of the sun. Adélies usually return to the same mates and nest sites every year. They lay eggs in November and by February the chicks go to sea.

Powerful oarlike flippers propel penguins through water

Stiff tail of pointed feathers used as rudder in water and as support on land

Torpedo-shaped body allows the penguin to slice through the water

Oily feathers overlap like roof tiles, providing a waterproof layer for the thick down feathers underneath

Adélie penguin *Pygoscelis adeliae*

Short legs are set far back on body for steering while swimming

PERFIDIOUS PENGUIN
An evil penguin stars in the Oscar-winning British animated film *The Wrong Trousers*. The treacherous penguin leaves a trail of havoc behind it as it attempts to remove a priceless jewel from a museum. Penguins are not, however, generally famed for their participation in diamond heists!

PADDED PENGUINS PARASCENDING
Tough feathers, a flexible skin, and thick blubber protect these penguins from knocks as they hurl themselves onto rocky shores or ice floes.

King penguin
*Aptenodytes
patagonica*

Gentoo penguin
Pygoscelis papua

Rockhopper penguin
*Eudyptes
chrysocome*

MARK OF DISTINCTION
The main distinguishing
marks of penguins are
on the head and upper
breast, so the birds are
visible when they swim
on the surface. The
colors and head crests
are used for species
recognition and for
courtship displays.

KING PENGUINS
Kings have golden-orange
patches on their ears and bill.
The long bill is useful for
catching speedy fish and squid.

GENTOO PENGUINS
The pink bill of gentoos is dagger-
shaped to catch fish and krill.
Gentoos can swim at speeds of
up to 16 miles (27 km) per hour.

ROCKHOPPER PENGUINS
Rockhoppers have conspicuous
yellow eyebrows that they use for
courtship display. They are the
smallest polar penguin.

NOISY NESTERS
Chinstrap penguins are good
climbers, using their beaks and
sharp claws to reach nest sites
in high rocky places. They are
noisy and aggressive penguins.
They often take over the
nesting sites of Adélies or
steal stones from one
another's nests.

CHICKS AT RISK
Weak and sickly chicks,
or those on the edge of the
colonies, are most likely to fall
victim to predators such as
the skua (right). In the
oceans, penguins
are prey to
leopard seals,
sea lions, and
killer whales.

*Black feathers
form a
"chinstrap"
across
white
breast*

*Shallow
nest
lined with
stones and
vegetation*

Chinstrap
penguin
*Pygoscelis
antarctica*

Emperors of the Antarctic

IN EARLY APRIL, when most of Antarctica's wildlife heads north, the emperor penguin begins its 60-mile (100-km) trek south to its traditional nesting sites on the sea ice. To reach the breeding colony, the birds must cover a huge area of sea ice in pitch darkness. In early May the female lays her egg and returns north to the open sea. The male then undertakes an incredible feat of endurance. During the icy winter he incubates the egg on his feet under a flap of warm skin. This means that for two months the male cannot feed, and may lose up to half his body weight. The female returns to feed the hatched chick in July. Each pair of emperors rears one chick a year, but only about one out of five survives.

FEET HEAT
Chicks stand on the adults' feet until they are about eight weeks old, hiding under a brood pouch, or flap of skin, for extra warmth and protection. Older chicks rely on their dense, fluffy feathers and the warm bodies of fellow chicks to keep them warm while their parents search for food.

TRULY MAJESTIC
The emperor, the largest penguin, stands nearly 4 ft (1.2 m) tall, and weighs 65 lb (30 kg). It can spend up to 18 minutes underwater and dive to over 850 ft (260 m).

The birds in the center are the warmest of the group

A tightly packed group can reduce heat loss by as much as 50 percent

Any bird that fails to join the huddle during the winter months faces certain death

Birds take turns occupying the most exposed positions

Emperors tend to turn their backs on the constantly shifting wind

TOGETHERNESS
Incubating males huddle together for warmth, moving very little in order to conserve energy. When the chicks are born the birds still huddle together as much as possible. Some emperor colonies contain over 20,000 pairs.

After the females return, the skinny and hungry males make their way to the open sea

Penguin "flies" out of the water to draw breath

Penguin catches fish and krill in its beak

Underwater, penguin steers with its feet and tail

Penguin shoots onto land or ice in giant leap of up to 6 ft (2 m)

DUCKING AND DIVING
Penguins "fly" through the water, propelled by their stiff flippers. When swimming fast, they often use a technique called porpoising, leaping out of the water like dolphins or porpoises. Air offers less resistance to movement than water, so porpoising penguins can travel at speeds of 18 miles (30 km) an hour.

Bill is small to cut
down on heat loss

Emperor penguin
Aptenodytes forsteri

In the nasal
cavities, much of
the warm air
that would
otherwise be lost
in breathing is
recycled

Closely packed,
overlapping
feathers cover a
thick layer of
blubber

Feet are small
to cut down on
heat loss

King of the Arctic

THE POLAR BEAR IS THE LARGEST and most powerful hunter of the Arctic lands; an average male weighs as much as six adult people. There are probably 20,000 polar bears wandering over the vast Arctic ice floes; some of them even roam as far as the North Pole. Polar bears are solitary animals except in the breeding season. They do not hibernate, and in the long winter, when the Arctic pack ice extends farther out to sea, they hunt for seals beneath the ice. Their dense fur keeps them warm even in the most severe conditions. An undercoat of thick fur is protected by an outer coat of long guard hairs. These hairs stick together when they get wet, forming a waterproof barrier. Under the fur, a thick layer of blubber performs two roles, insulating the bear against the cold and acting as a food store to help the bear survive hard times.

The small rounded ears lose little body heat

HEAVYWEIGHT
An average adult male polar bear measures 8 ft (2.5 m) from head to tail and weighs over 1,000 lb (about 500 kg). The largest males grow up to 10 ft (3 m) in length and can weigh up to 2,000 lb (900 kg). Female polar bears are much smaller than the males.

Female keeps floor clean by covering it with freshly scraped snow

Air vent scraped in roof lets stale air escape

Female first digs the tunnel, then hollows out the chamber

Strong teeth for killing prey

BEARING ARMS
By playing, cubs gain strength and practice skills they will need when they are adults. Young bears often wrestle in the snow with their mouths wide open to show off their sharp teeth. Such fights rarely result in injury. Finding and killing prey is not easy, and bears have developed a bad reputation for raiding human settlements in search of food.

CAVE CUBS
Polar bear cubs are born in December or January in a warm cozy den dug in the snow by the mother. The cubs grow rapidly on their mother's rich milk, which is about 30 percent fat. While in the ice cave, the mother has nothing to eat and lives on the stored fat in her body.

CAPABLE CLIMBER
In spite of their huge size, polar bears are able to climb trees, such as this one at Cape Churchill on Hudson Bay in Canada. Between 600 and 1,000 bears gather here in October to wait for the bay to freeze over so that they can head out over the ice to hunt.

Thick fur prevents bear from being scratched

Back legs are especially strong

POLAR PADDLE
Polar bears are slow but very strong swimmers, able to keep swimming for a long time. The bears use only their front legs to propel themselves; the back legs are held still like a rudder.

SEAL SLAYER
Polar bears are clever and patient hunters. Over 90 percent of their diet consists of seals. They wait by a seal's blowhole in the ice, pouncing as soon as it comes up for air. One stroke of the bear's massive paw and a bite at the back of the skull kill the seal. But most hunting trips are unsuccessful, and a bear may not eat for five days.

Yellow-white fur acts as camouflage

Powerful legs to outrun prey

Hollow hairs trap warm air near body

Thickly padded soles covered by rough skin and sometimes tough hair

Sharp claws for grabbing prey

Non-slip soles help grip slippery ice

Flat shape gives moose a stable surface with which to push rivals

The mighty moose

THE MOOSE IS THE LARGEST MEMBER of the deer family. It stands up to 7.5 ft (2.4 m) tall and can weigh up to 1,800 lb (825 kg). The moose can be found throughout the northern United States and Canada, and in northern Europe and Asia, where it is sometimes called elk. In Europe and Asia the moose lives mainly in the coniferous forests bordering the tundra, but in North America it ranges widely over the tundra, spending long periods on the shores of the Arctic ocean in midsummer, when flies are likely to plague it farther inland. When winters are particularly harsh, moose often move farther south in search of food, to areas that have lighter snow cover. Moose are solitary animals and their population density is low; because of their immense size they need a relatively large area to themselves to enable them to find an adequate food supply. However, in winter, when in search of new food supplies, they will often travel in a group, covering considerable distances.

The bell is a fold of skin covered with hair

LETHAL WEAPONS
The bull moose has heavy, flat antlers. It uses them more for fighting rival males during the breeding season than for protection. The moose sheds its antlers every year and grows a new set. By late August the antlers are fully grown, and the bull strips off the "velvet" covering and polishes his great weapons against a tree.

Undersurface of moose's foot

SURE-FOOTED
The moose has long and sharply pointed hooves, in contrast to those of its relative, the reindeer, which are rounded. The pointed hooves help the moose grip ice and snow.

Moose
Alces alces

Calf remains close to mother for several months

Reddish-brown coat becomes darker as the calf matures

Long legs allow even young moose to walk easily through deep snow

MAKING MORE MOOSE
The mating season of the moose lasts from four to eight weeks in the fall. The bull wanders around looking for and calling to females (cows); the cows return the calls. The bull will follow every sound to see if it was made by a cow or a rival bull. Baby moose are born in late May and June. The mother carries the baby for about seven and a half months before the birth. There is usually one calf, although twins and even triplets are not uncommon. When the calf is about ten days old, it can travel with its mother.

Antler spread can be as much as 6 ft 8 in (2.05 m)

Antlers are not fully grown and are still heavily covered with velvet

MONEY MOOSE
The moose is such a revered animal in many northern European countries that it has even been featured on banknotes. This note comes from Lithuania.

Muzzle hangs 3–4 in (8–10 cm) over its chin

Short neck, coupled with long legs, means that moose has to get on its knees to eat low-growing plants

Arctic willow *Salix arctica*

FAVORITE FOOD
Arctic willow (*Salix arctica*) and Alaska willow (*Salix alaxensis*) are the favorite foods of the moose.

SOLITARY GIANT
The preferred habitat of moose is tundra land containing willow swamps and lakes. Moose are good swimmers and can cross lakes and rivers with ease. They like to roll in mud holes, which helps them to get rid of any small parasitic animals. In summer, they eat leaves and tender twigs as well as grass and herbs. Because of their great size and dangerous antlers they have few natural predators, with the exception of humans. Wolves may occasionally attack isolated moose and the young, although the antlers of the adult make it a formidable foe.

Moose is beginning to lose the velvet on its antlers

WATER WADERS
Moose are often to be found standing up to their knees in water. This helps them to get rid of the flies that trouble them greatly in the warm summer months, but they also feed on the aquatic vegetation. An adult will consume up to 43 lb (19.5 kg) of vegetation a day. Sometimes they retreat into water to escape predators such as wolves.

Tundra wildlife

THE ONLY ANIMAL that can live on the Arctic pack ice is the polar bear. However, several animals live on the Arctic tundra (pp. 8–9), both as residents and migrants. During summer in the Arctic a great deal of the ice on the tundra melts, plants begin to flourish, and insect eggs hatch. This means that suddenly there is plenty of food for animals that have spent all winter on the tundra, as well as for the migrants who arrive as soon as the snows melt. Because the sun never sets in the Arctic in summer (pp. 6–7), the animals can feed all through the night. It is necessary for them to do this so that the young can grow as quickly as possible, because the summer is short and the land soon freezes over again.

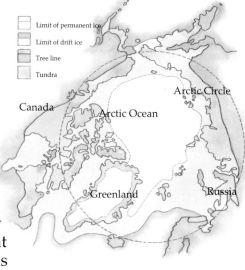

Limit of permanent ice
Limit of drift ice
Tree line
Tundra

Canada
Arctic Ocean
Arctic Circle
Greenland
Russia

TUNDRA VEGETATION
The tundra consists of a nearly continuous, though at times thin, cover of vegetation, dominated by grasses like the Arctic cottongrass (*Eriophorum angustifolium*) seen here. Scattered among the grasses are various mosses, a variety of flowering herbs, and a few species of dwarf shrubs and willows.

SEA OF ICE
The central area of the Arctic Ocean remains permanently frozen. The tundra, which spans North America and Eurasia, is covered in snow and ice in winter but is green in summer. No trees grow on the tundra because it is too cold and windy, even in the summer months.

Long, pointed ears enable the lynx to hear well in dense, muffling snow

FELINE VISITOR
The Arctic lynx (*Lynx canadensis*) is mainly a creature of the forest that borders areas of the tundra in North America, but they are often found in the true tundra during the summer months. Their brown coat blends well with the tundra landscape in summer, and in winter the coat becomes thicker and lighter so that the lynx is hard to see against the snow.

In winter big feet are covered with thick fur that acts like a snowshoe

Snowshoe hare
Lepus americanus

HARE LINE
Three types of hares inhabit the tundra – the snowshoe hare, the rare Alaskan hare, and the common Arctic hare. Hares grow white winter coats and have well-developed claws that enable them to dig through the snow for food.

The lemming is very common on the tundra

MASS SUICIDE?
Every few years, when their numbers outgrow their food source, lemmings (*Lemmus sibiricus*) become restless and a mass migration begins. They press on madly, often passing food sources, until they reach the sea, where hundreds drown.

TURNCOAT
The stoat (*Mustela erminea*) is protected from harsh weather in its home beneath the snow. It is often called "ermine" when its coat is in its white winter phase. It is a cute-looking animal, but a ruthless hunter. The stoat's slimness enables it to pursue lemmings, its main prey, through the lemmings' networks of underground tunnels.

GREAT BEAR
The word "Arctic" comes from the Greek word *Arctikos*, meaning "pertaining to the constellation of the bear." The extensive star constellation Ursa Major, the Great Bear, is visible only in the northern hemisphere.

GLUTTON OF THE ARCTIC
The wolverine (*Gulo gulo*), a distant relative of the stoat, looks like a small bear. Wolverines are solitary animals and usually meet others only to mate during the summer. They are relentless hunters, able to pursue their victims for many miles without tiring. Their main prey is reindeer. After a kill, much of the flesh is eaten on the spot, but they hide the remainder for another day, earning themselves a reputation for gluttony. Wolverine fur is much prized.

Sometimes the fur is tipped silvery white

Bears have sensitive noses and a strong sense of smell

Powerful jaws and teeth allow bear to eat a variety of foods

SLEEPYHEAD
The brown or grizzly bear (*Ursus arctos*) lives in the tundra regions of Alaska and Canada and in some parts of Russia. They eat a wide variety of small mammals, fish, insects, and plants, depending on the season and the area in which they live. In the winter months the grizzly digs a snug den in the ground and hibernates, taking approximately two weeks to enter a deep winter sleep. During hibernation the body temperature drops and the bear lives off its reserves of stored fat. It sometimes sleeps for as long as seven months.

Long claws on the front paws help the bear to dig

Bears often stand upright on the soles of their back feet

Reindeer and caribou

Rᴇɪɴᴅᴇᴇʀ ᴀʀᴇ ᴄᴀʟʟᴇᴅ ᴄᴀʀɪʙᴏᴜ in North America. The name "caribou" may come from *xalibu*, the Native American Micmac word for "the animal that paws through snow for its food." Wild reindeer still survive on the frozen tundra of North America, Siberia, and Scandinavia, but they have also been domesticated in Scandinavia and Siberia for thousands of years. Although their thick coats insulate them against the Arctic cold, they migrate south in the winter to find food and shelter. As they travel, their coats grow thick and gray. In summer, reindeer are plagued by hordes of insects, such as mosquitoes and warble flies, as they graze on the tundra meadows. Their main predator is the wolf; this natural population regulation is necessary to enable the surviving reindeer to find sufficient food in a decreasing habitat.

REINDEER STAR
The most famous reindeer in the world is probably red-nosed Rudolph, the reindeer who leads Santa Claus's sleigh.

Antler buds appear two weeks after the old ones are shed

New antlers are covered by soft, thick velvet

Fully formed antlers are bone-hard

TITLE FIGHT
In the fall rutting, or mating, season, bulls with their antlers locked together wrestle to decide which is the strongest. The winner of these contests collects a group of cows for mating and then defends his harem from all challengers.

BIG, BIGGER, BIGGEST
Antlers are shed each year. Bulls shed their antlers at the end of the year, but the cows wait until spring. New antlers grow rapidly and are fully grown by the start of the fall rutting season.

Nuclear explosion

NUCLEAR POLLUTION
In 1986 a nuclear reactor at Chernobyl in Ukraine exploded. Lichens and mosses absorbed radioactive Cesium 137. Reindeer ate the lichens, making them ill and their meat unfit to eat.

Reindeer moss (*Cladonia* species) absorbed radioactivity from the air

Velvet contains blood vessels to nourish the growing antlers

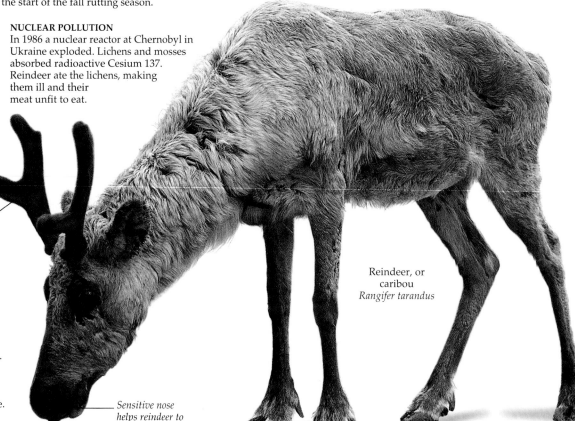

Reindeer, or caribou
Rangifer tarandus

LICHEN LUNCH
Reindeer feed largely on lichens, which are one of the few foods available throughout the Arctic winter. Some reindeer living on Arctic islands will also eat seaweed. In summer a wider variety of plants are available. Adult reindeer eat about 10 lb (4.5 kg) of food a day to get the energy they need.

Sensitive nose helps reindeer to find food even under the snow

CEREMONIAL APRON

This shaman's ceremonial apron was made from reindeer hide. The shaman was a powerful figure in the culture of many native Siberian and North American peoples. It was believed he could get power from supernatural beings that were everywhere on land, and even lurked beneath the sea.

Iron symbols of the sun, fish, and diving birds decorate apron

Heat is lost rapidly through antlers in velvet, cooling the reindeer on hot summer days

Hollow hairs contain air that traps body heat

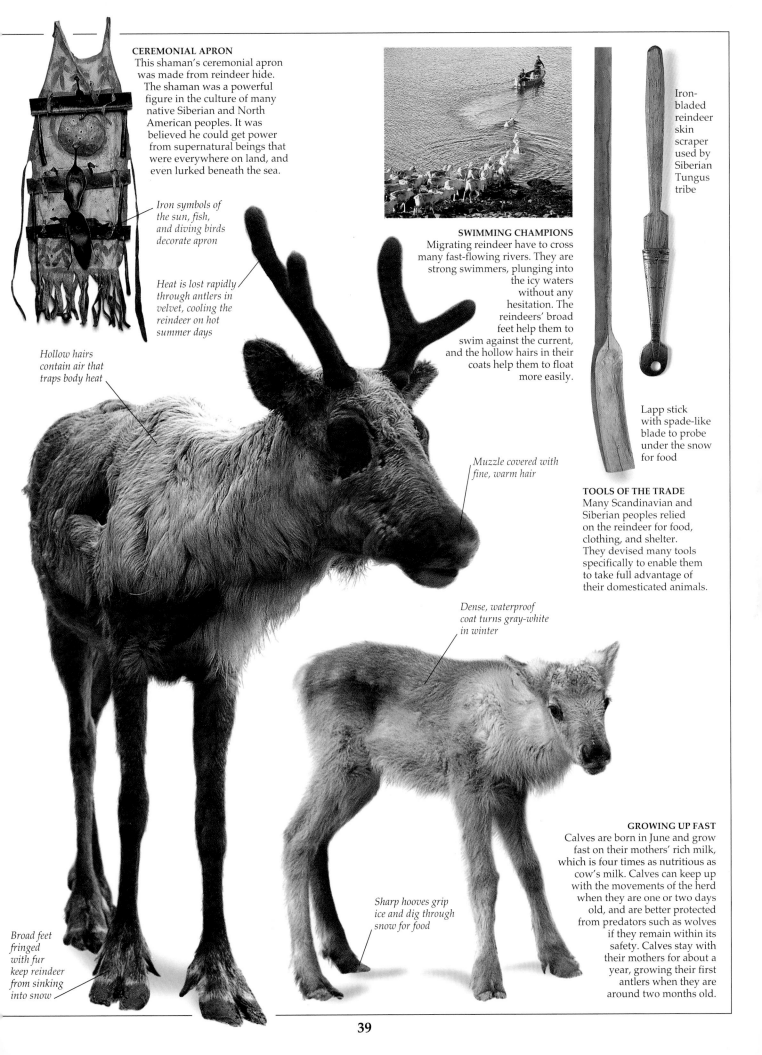

Iron-bladed reindeer skin scraper used by Siberian Tungus tribe

SWIMMING CHAMPIONS

Migrating reindeer have to cross many fast-flowing rivers. They are strong swimmers, plunging into the icy waters without any hesitation. The reindeers' broad feet help them to swim against the current, and the hollow hairs in their coats help them to float more easily.

Lapp stick with spade-like blade to probe under the snow for food

TOOLS OF THE TRADE

Many Scandinavian and Siberian peoples relied on the reindeer for food, clothing, and shelter. They devised many tools specifically to enable them to take full advantage of their domesticated animals.

Muzzle covered with fine, warm hair

Dense, waterproof coat turns gray-white in winter

Sharp hooves grip ice and dig through snow for food

Broad feet fringed with fur keep reindeer from sinking into snow

GROWING UP FAST

Calves are born in June and grow fast on their mothers' rich milk, which is four times as nutritious as cow's milk. Calves can keep up with the movements of the herd when they are one or two days old, and are better protected from predators such as wolves if they remain within its safety. Calves stay with their mothers for about a year, growing their first antlers when they are around two months old.

Company of wolves

BLENDING INTO THE BACKGROUND
In the Arctic areas of North America and Eurasia, wolves often have white coats for camouflage. Because the animals they hunt cannot see them easily, the wolves can get very close to their prey. In the forests to the south of the tundra, the wolves have gray or even blackish fur.

WOLVES ARE INTELLIGENT AND ADAPTABLE animals that survive in the Arctic cold thanks to their thick fur and cooperative hunting techniques. They generally live in packs of between 8 and 20 family members. They are bonded together by affection for each other, and by a ranking system of near-military precision. Pack members establish their rank at almost every meeting: a dominant or high-ranking wolf stands erect, ears and tail pointing upward, and may show its teeth, then growl. A subordinate or low-ranking wolf crouches, holds its tail between its legs, and turns down its ears; instead of growling, it whines. A wolf pack ranges over a specific area, picking off sick, aged, or injured herd animals. Needlessly feared and persecuted by humans for thousands of years, wolves kill only to survive, and do not deserve their bad reputation – they are, in fact, the ancestors of all domesticated dogs.

RING OF HORN
Wolves are expert hunters and prey chiefly on large hooved animals such as caribou, moose, and musk oxen. To defend themselves from a wolf pack, a herd of musk oxen forms a tight circle, with the wolves on the outside and the females and young in the center. By panicking the musk oxen, the wolves can break the circle and reach the calves inside. But if a wolf is caught by one of the musk oxen's horns, it can be tossed into the air and then trampled.

Mouth remains wide open during howling

Wolf throws back its head in order to howl

Wolf
Canis lupus

LEADER OF THE PACK
The wolf's instinct for power and freedom has inspired countless writers. The American novelist Jack London wrote his novel *The Call of the Wild* after spending a year in the Yukon in Canada. It is the story of Buck, a domestic dog who becomes wild and eventually leads a wolf pack.

IN HARMONY
An eerie howl in the night echoes through countless horror films, striking terror into the hearts of the audience. In fact, howling is simply one of the ways in which wolves communicate with one another. Wolf-speak ranges from whimpers and growls to complex facial and body expressions. Wolves howl in order to keep in touch with pack members, or to warn other packs to keep out of the area. If one wolf howls, the others join in, often harmonizing with each other. The variety of sound makes the pack seem bigger and more formidable.

Sensitive ears can track sounds
up to 2 miles (3 km) away

Wolves have as
many as 17
different facial
expressions

Poor eyesight means wolves
must rely on superb hearing
and sense of smell

Long muzzle hides powerful jaws
and teeth for killing prey and
tearing flesh; 42 teeth include
sharp canines for gripping prey

Two-layered coat with soft,
dense underfur and long outer
hairs to keep out the cold

THE WOLF WITHIN
Jack London's novel *White Fang*,
set in the Yukon Territory, is
the story of a wolf domesticated
to become a pet. In practice, it
is virtually impossible – and
illegal – to keep wild
wolves as pets.

BORN TO BE WILD
Wolves are superbly adapted to Arctic life.
Their keen sense of smell and hearing has
been honed to perfection for tracking down
their prey. They have evolved strong bodies
and long legs for chasing their quarry. Agile
and graceful, they can jump up to 15 ft
(4.5 m) and can leap upward, sideways,
and even backward, like a cat. Just like dogs,
wolves walk on their toes and have large
pads with claws that do not retract. This
allows them to run fast on flat ground while
keeping their footing on rocks, ice, and other
slippery surfaces.

Wolves can sleep out in the
open tundra, although they
often find a snow hole or a
cave in which to shelter

Gray wolf
Canis lupus

The weighty walrus

Huge, ungainly, and enormously fat, the walrus, a close relative of the seal, has adapted superbly to its Arctic lifestyle. A thick layer of blubber (fat) keeps the animal warm. Its four flat flippers make the walrus an excellent swimmer, as well as allowing it to shift its heavy bulk on land. Female walruses give birth in the spring, usually on boulder-strewn beaches. The female usually produces one calf every other year, and cares for her young for about two years – twins are very rare. Walruses follow the seasonal ebb and flow of the Arctic ice, migrating as far as 1,800 miles (3,000 km) north each year. In the process, the animals must evade polar bears and killer whales, their greatest enemies other than humans.

WORLD-FAMOUS WALRUS
Lewis Carroll (1832–98) included a walrus and a carpenter in his famous story *Alice Through the Looking Glass*. They invite some oysters to walk with them – and then eat them. In real life, walruses do eat mainly shellfish, such as clams and mussels.

THE CALL OF LOVE
Walrus courtship is an elaborate process. A male seduces a female with barks, growls, and whistles. If she is impressed by his love song, she will slip off with him and mate in the water. These two walruses are tenderly rubbing mustaches prior to mating.

Thick skin on neck and shoulders protects the walrus during fights

FURRY FRIEND
Just like the much smaller catfish, walruses have a row of coarse but very sensitive whiskers. The whiskers grow constantly to make up for daily wear and tear. The walrus uses the delicate mustache to search for invertebrates on the murky ocean floor.

Broad front flippers can support heavy body on land

Walrus
Odobenus rosmarus

HEAVYWEIGHT
Weighing in at around 2,200 lb (1 tonne), this formidable male walrus surveys his domain. Females are only slightly smaller, weighing about 1,900 lb (0.85 tonne).

AN INTIMATE ARRANGEMENT
Walruses are extremely sociable animals. During the summer, enormous groups of walruses lie around on the land, packed together in large, noisy groups. Keeping close together conserves body heat, as well as making it harder for a predator to pick off an individual animal.

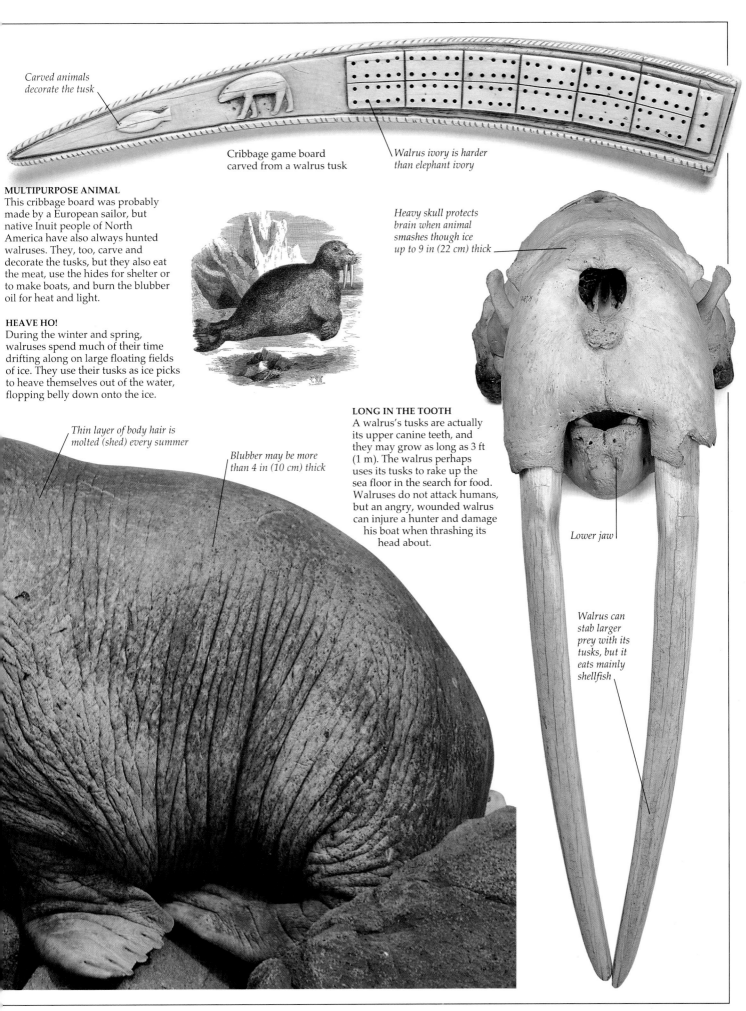

Carved animals decorate the tusk

Cribbage game board carved from a walrus tusk

Walrus ivory is harder than elephant ivory

MULTIPURPOSE ANIMAL
This cribbage board was probably made by a European sailor, but native Inuit people of North America have also always hunted walruses. They, too, carve and decorate the tusks, but they also eat the meat, use the hides for shelter or to make boats, and burn the blubber oil for heat and light.

HEAVE HO!
During the winter and spring, walruses spend much of their time drifting along on large floating fields of ice. They use their tusks as ice picks to heave themselves out of the water, flopping belly down onto the ice.

Heavy skull protects brain when animal smashes though ice up to 9 in (22 cm) thick

Thin layer of body hair is molted (shed) every summer

Blubber may be more than 4 in (10 cm) thick

LONG IN THE TOOTH
A walrus's tusks are actually its upper canine teeth, and they may grow as long as 3 ft (1 m). The walrus perhaps uses its tusks to rake up the sea floor in the search for food. Walruses do not attack humans, but an angry, wounded walrus can injure a hunter and damage his boat when thrashing its head about.

Lower jaw

Walrus can stab larger prey with its tusks, but it eats mainly shellfish

Suited to the sea

SEALS ARE PROBABLY the hardiest of all the Arctic and Antarctic mammals. The ringed seal of the Arctic and the Weddell seal of the Antarctic both survive below the ice during the dark winter months. Other seals, such as the Arctic harp seal, migrate into polar waters as the warmer summer weather arrives. All seals have to leave the water to rest, give birth, and mate. In contrast to their graceful swimming in the sea, seals move clumsily on land, wriggling and sliding across the ice with some difficulty. Seals usually give birth in late winter. By spring the pups are strong enough to start making the most of the fish and rich food supplies of the polar waters. Fur seals and sea lions have problems coping with the heat of an Arctic or Antarctic summer. Their fur and blubber causes them to overheat, and the seals have to pant, flap their flippers, or cover their bodies with sand or mud to cool down. Seals have been hunted for their fur and blubber for hundreds of years; they are also threatened by the increasing pollution of the oceans.

Guard hairs protect the seal as it slides over rocks on land

Dense underfur traps a layer of warm air and keeps seal warm

TWO FUR COATS
Fur seals have two kinds of hair in their coat. Long guard hairs on the outside form a protective layer, and fine underfur keeps body heat from escaping. Other seals have hairless bodies, and depend on their blubber for warmth.

ICY WINTERS
Weddell seals (*Leptonychotes weddelli*) spend the whole winter under the Antarctic ice sheet, gnawing at the ice with their teeth to keep air holes open for breathing. In summer, the seals move onto the ice or rocks. Pups are born in September or October, and can swim at about six weeks. Weddell seals make a wide range of sounds underwater, possibly for locating prey or blowholes, or to communicate with other seals. They can dive to depths of about 1,900 ft (580 m), and stay submerged for up to 70 minutes.

BALLOON NOSE
Male hooded seals (*Cystophora cristata*) have an inflatable balloon-like structure at the end of their nose. It is blown up when the seal is excited or in danger, and may serve to warn off rivals or enemies.

The male has a huge swollen nose like an elephant's trunk

JOBS FOR THE BOYS
Gigantic male southern elephant seals (*Mirounga leonina*) roar defiance to their rivals in the breeding season, using their extraordinary nose like a loudspeaker. The female gives birth to a single pup, which she nurses for about a month. During this period she will not feed, existing instead on energy reserves in her blubber. Males do not eat during the breeding season either, since they are constantly defending a harem of females against rival males.

Male elephant seals are up to ten times heavier than females

HIDDEN DEATH
Inuit hunters sometimes hide behind white shields mounted on small sleds as they hunt seals.

While it is nursed the pup may quadruple its weight in three to four weeks.

Cusps on cheek teeth filter food

Cranium

TRIDENT TEETH
The crabeater seal (*Lobodon carcinophagus*) does not eat crabs. It uses its trident-shaped teeth to strain shrimplike krill from Antarctic waters. The crabeater swims at great speed with its mouth open, forcing the water through spaces in its teeth. Between five and eight million crabeater seals live in the Antarctic; they have few enemies, other than killer whales.

Huge mouth can gape wide open and snap shut to grasp prey

Powerful canine teeth for stripping flesh

BUILT FOR A PURPOSE
A seal limb looks very different from a human foot. Under the skin, however, the bones are the same, adapted over millions of years to their different functions. A seal limb has been modified to form a webbed paddle. True seals use their back flippers to swim through the water; fur seals and sea lions use their front flippers instead, keeping the back flippers as a rudder for steering.

Fibula

Lower leg bones

Tibia

Ankle bone

Ankle bone

Foot bones

Sole bones

Toe bones

Toe bones

Human foot

Seal flipper

Large eyes to find prey underwater

SEAL THERAPY
When the strains of underwater life become too much, most seals, such as this leopard seal, hoist themselves up onto the ice for a rest and some sunbathing.

SPOTTED HUNTER
The aggressive leopard seal (*Hydrurga leptonyx*) is named for the large dark spots on its skin. These slender animals are built for speed, and have a long, flexible neck and a wide mouth for grasping penguins, seal pups, and other prey. Leopard seals pursue penguins underwater, then carry their victims to the surface, where they beat them against the water, turning them inside out to remove the skin, before gulping them down. The seal may spend up to an hour slowly eating in this way.

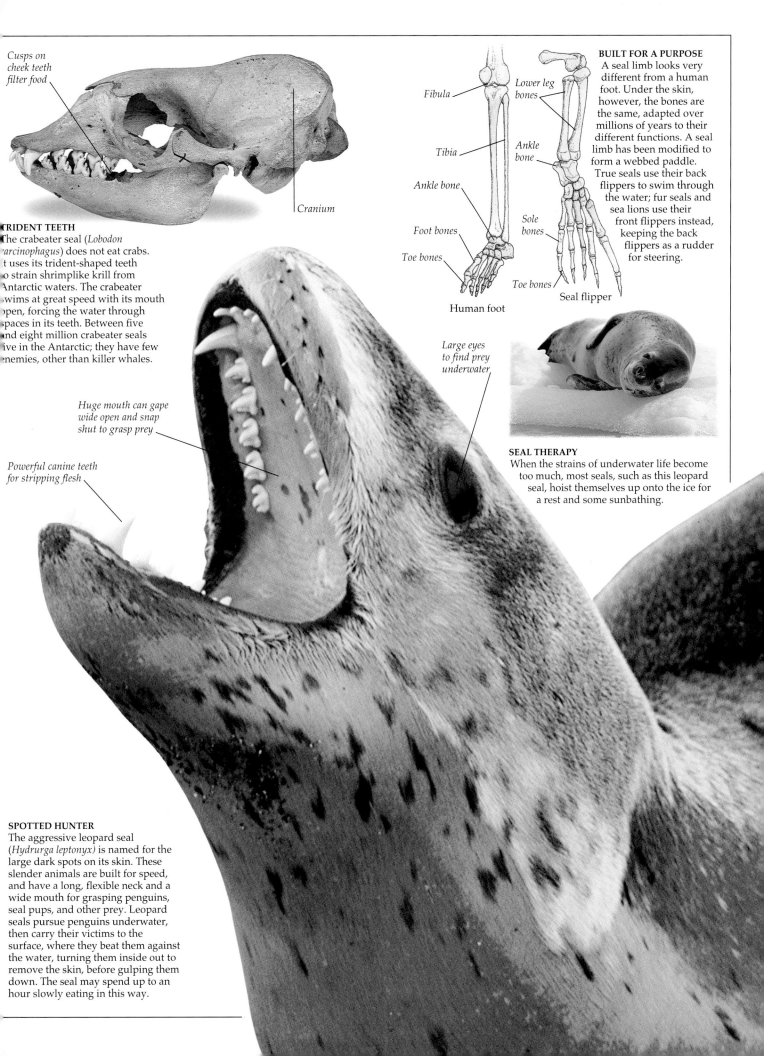

Giants of the seas

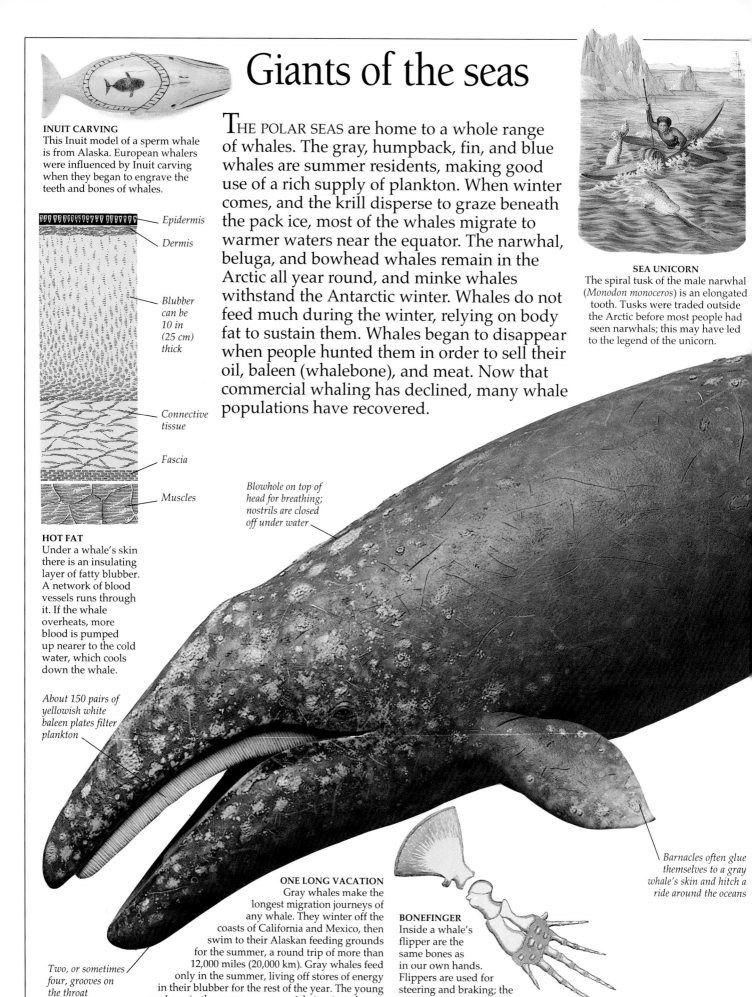

THE POLAR SEAS are home to a whole range of whales. The gray, humpback, fin, and blue whales are summer residents, making good use of a rich supply of plankton. When winter comes, and the krill disperse to graze beneath the pack ice, most of the whales migrate to warmer waters near the equator. The narwhal, beluga, and bowhead whales remain in the Arctic all year round, and minke whales withstand the Antarctic winter. Whales do not feed much during the winter, relying on body fat to sustain them. Whales began to disappear when people hunted them in order to sell their oil, baleen (whalebone), and meat. Now that commercial whaling has declined, many whale populations have recovered.

INUIT CARVING
This Inuit model of a sperm whale is from Alaska. European whalers were influenced by Inuit carving when they began to engrave the teeth and bones of whales.

Epidermis

Dermis

Blubber can be 10 in (25 cm) thick

Connective tissue

Fascia

Muscles

HOT FAT
Under a whale's skin there is an insulating layer of fatty blubber. A network of blood vessels runs through it. If the whale overheats, more blood is pumped up nearer to the cold water, which cools down the whale.

About 150 pairs of yellowish white baleen plates filter plankton

SEA UNICORN
The spiral tusk of the male narwhal (*Monodon monoceros*) is an elongated tooth. Tusks were traded outside the Arctic before most people had seen narwhals; this may have led to the legend of the unicorn.

Blowhole on top of head for breathing; nostrils are closed off under water

ONE LONG VACATION
Gray whales make the longest migration journeys of any whale. They winter off the coasts of California and Mexico, then swim to their Alaskan feeding grounds for the summer, a round trip of more than 12,000 miles (20,000 km). Gray whales feed only in the summer, living off stores of energy in their blubber for the rest of the year. The young are born in the warmer waters of their winter home.

BONEFINGER
Inside a whale's flipper are the same bones as in our own hands. Flippers are used for steering and braking; the tail provides swimming power.

Barnacles often glue themselves to a gray whale's skin and hitch a ride around the oceans

Two, or sometimes four, grooves on the throat

46

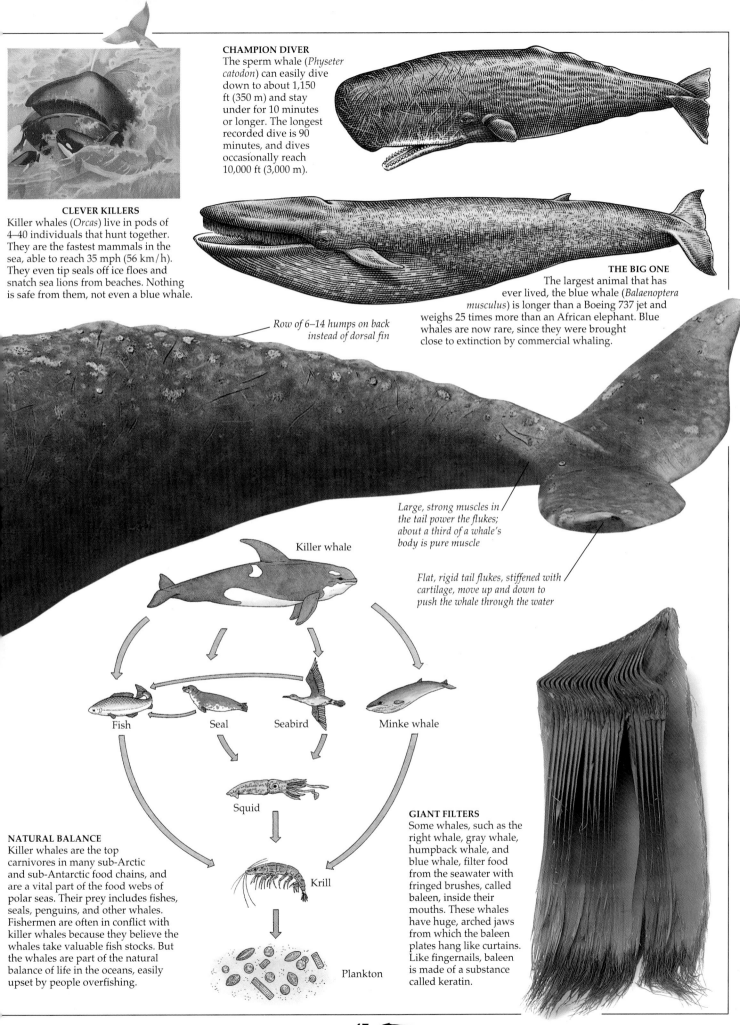

CHAMPION DIVER
The sperm whale (*Physeter catodon*) can easily dive down to about 1,150 ft (350 m) and stay under for 10 minutes or longer. The longest recorded dive is 90 minutes, and dives occasionally reach 10,000 ft (3,000 m).

CLEVER KILLERS
Killer whales (*Orcas*) live in pods of 4–40 individuals that hunt together. They are the fastest mammals in the sea, able to reach 35 mph (56 km/h). They even tip seals off ice floes and snatch sea lions from beaches. Nothing is safe from them, not even a blue whale.

THE BIG ONE
The largest animal that has ever lived, the blue whale (*Balaenoptera musculus*) is longer than a Boeing 737 jet and weighs 25 times more than an African elephant. Blue whales are now rare, since they were brought close to extinction by commercial whaling.

Row of 6–14 humps on back instead of dorsal fin

Large, strong muscles in the tail power the flukes; about a third of a whale's body is pure muscle

Flat, rigid tail flukes, stiffened with cartilage, move up and down to push the whale through the water

Killer whale

Fish Seal Seabird Minke whale

Squid

Krill

Plankton

NATURAL BALANCE
Killer whales are the top carnivores in many sub-Arctic and sub-Antarctic food chains, and are a vital part of the food webs of polar seas. Their prey includes fishes, seals, penguins, and other whales. Fishermen are often in conflict with killer whales because they believe the whales take valuable fish stocks. But the whales are part of the natural balance of life in the oceans, easily upset by people overfishing.

GIANT FILTERS
Some whales, such as the right whale, gray whale, humpback whale, and blue whale, filter food from the seawater with fringed brushes, called baleen, inside their mouths. These whales have huge, arched jaws from which the baleen plates hang like curtains. Like fingernails, baleen is made of a substance called keratin.

A herding life

PEOPLE HAVE SURVIVED in the inhospitable Arctic regions of northern Scandinavia and the northern regions of Siberia for thousands of years. Native Arctic peoples followed a nomadic (traveling) hunting and fishing lifestyle, adapting to the intense winter cold, darkness, and snow without the aid of modern technology. Starvation and death by exposure were constant threats. Native peoples of the Eurasian Arctic include the Saami, or Lapps, of northern Scandinavia, and the Chukchi, Evenks, and Nenets of Siberia and northeastern Asia. Some Chukchi families still follow wild reindeer herds, hunting or lassoing them for their meat and pelts. Reindeer provided Arctic peoples with all their basic needs – food, clothing, tents, tools, and items to trade. In some remote areas, the native peoples still follow a traditional hunting lifestyle. But many now work in villages or towns, and some combine the old and new ways of life.

Staff is made of iron

Foot represents a bear's paw

SPIRIT POWER
In many traditional Siberian societies, a specially trained *angakok*, or shaman, acted as the link between the supernatural and natural worlds. A shaman fulfilled many roles, from doctor and meteorologist to performer of miracles. This shaman's headdress is embroidered with reindeer hair.

Shaman's head ornament from the Ostyak-Nenet tribe of Siberia

HANDY IN WINTER
This ivory carving of reindeer pulling a sled comes from central Siberia. Many Siberian tribes used reindeer as pack and draft (pulling) animals for carrying their household goods. Today, some reindeer herders hire out their reindeer sleds for transportation during the winter.

Bag is made of stretched reindeer hide

Hide from different parts of the reindeer's body provides the bag's decoration

IN A TRANCE
Shamans of the Tungus tribe, east of the Yenisey River in central Siberia, held this staff while meditating. The shaman often went into a trance and spoke with the voice of a spirit "helper."

PACK YOUR BAG
The northern Komi lived to the west of the Ural Mountains, in northeastern Europe. They filled this *patku*, or knapsack, with clothes and other smaller items, and loaded it onto a baggage sled when following reindeer herds.

MOVING CAMP
Because nomadic people often moved several times a year, their tents had to be simple and lightweight as well as sturdy. The tents usually had a conical framework of wooden poles, covered with several reindeer skins. The top of the tent was left open to allow smoke from the fire to escape.

Nenet tent, Siberia

A great deal of heat is lost through the head, so a hood is vital for keeping the head and ears warm in freezing conditions

Seams are very finely stitched to make the garment as warm and waterproof as possible

Nenet child's hooded winter parka

HUNTER OR HUNTED?
This hooded jacket from the Aleutian islands, between Siberia and Alaska, is made from strips of seal or walrus intestine, sewn together to make a waterproof garment. By dressing in the skins or fur of the animals, the hunter was making an important point – he became part of the animal world around him by taking on the appearance of the hunted.

Reindeer gut was often used for sewing skins together

Mittens are sewn right into the sleeves for extra warmth and protection

Fur trim was decorative, but also protected against icy winds

ORIGINS OF THE PARKA
The traditional winter coat of the Nenet tribe of northern Siberia consisted of a thick, warm long-sleeved jacket called a parka. The coat was sewn together from pieces of reindeer skin. The reindeer hide was worn on the outside; for the inner clothing, softer fur was placed next to the skin for extra warmth. Woolen undergarments provided added protection, and helped to trap body heat. Some people still wear traditional clothes, but most buy winter clothes made of synthetic materials.

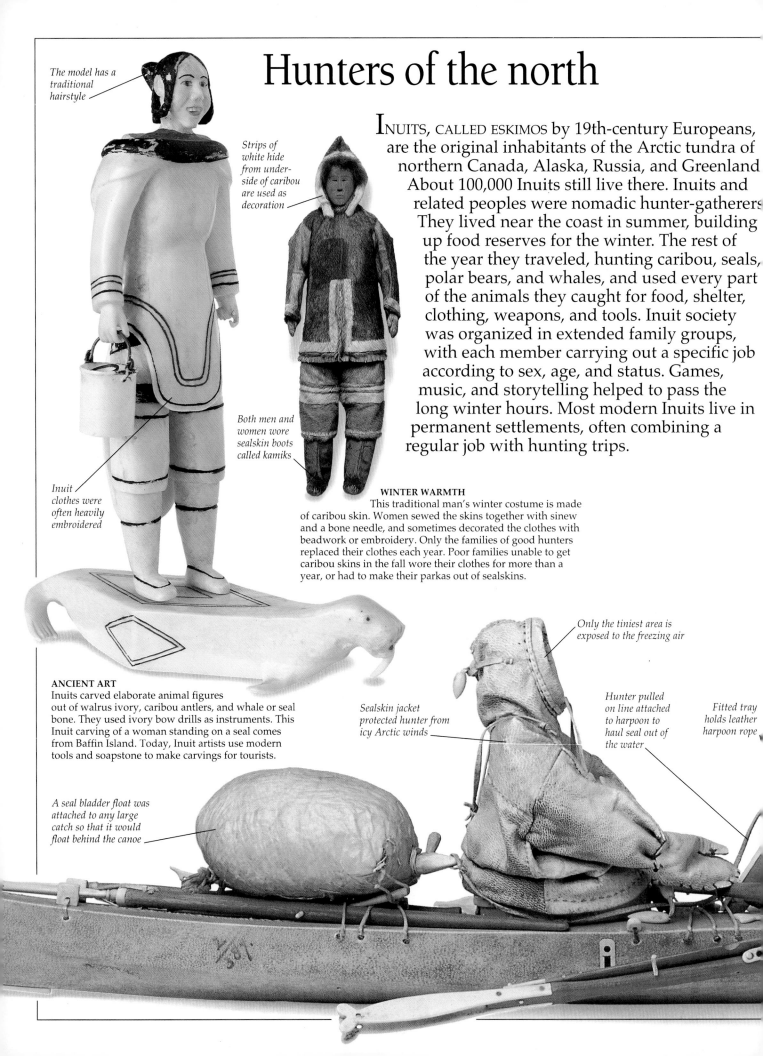

Hunters of the north

The model has a traditional hairstyle

Strips of white hide from underside of caribou are used as decoration

Both men and women wore sealskin boots called kamiks

Inuit clothes were often heavily embroidered

INUITS, CALLED ESKIMOS by 19th-century Europeans, are the original inhabitants of the Arctic tundra of northern Canada, Alaska, Russia, and Greenland About 100,000 Inuits still live there. Inuits and related peoples were nomadic hunter-gatherers They lived near the coast in summer, building up food reserves for the winter. The rest of the year they traveled, hunting caribou, seals, polar bears, and whales, and used every part of the animals they caught for food, shelter, clothing, weapons, and tools. Inuit society was organized in extended family groups, with each member carrying out a specific job according to sex, age, and status. Games, music, and storytelling helped to pass the long winter hours. Most modern Inuits live in permanent settlements, often combining a regular job with hunting trips.

WINTER WARMTH
This traditional man's winter costume is made of caribou skin. Women sewed the skins together with sinew and a bone needle, and sometimes decorated the clothes with beadwork or embroidery. Only the families of good hunters replaced their clothes each year. Poor families unable to get caribou skins in the fall wore their clothes for more than a year, or had to make their parkas out of sealskins.

ANCIENT ART
Inuits carved elaborate animal figures out of walrus ivory, caribou antlers, and whale or seal bone. They used ivory bow drills as instruments. This Inuit carving of a woman standing on a seal comes from Baffin Island. Today, Inuit artists use modern tools and soapstone to make carvings for tourists.

Only the tiniest area is exposed to the freezing air

Hunter pulled on line attached to harpoon to haul seal out of the water

Fitted tray holds leather harpoon rope

Sealskin jacket protected hunter from icy Arctic winds

A seal bladder float was attached to any large catch so that it would float behind the canoe

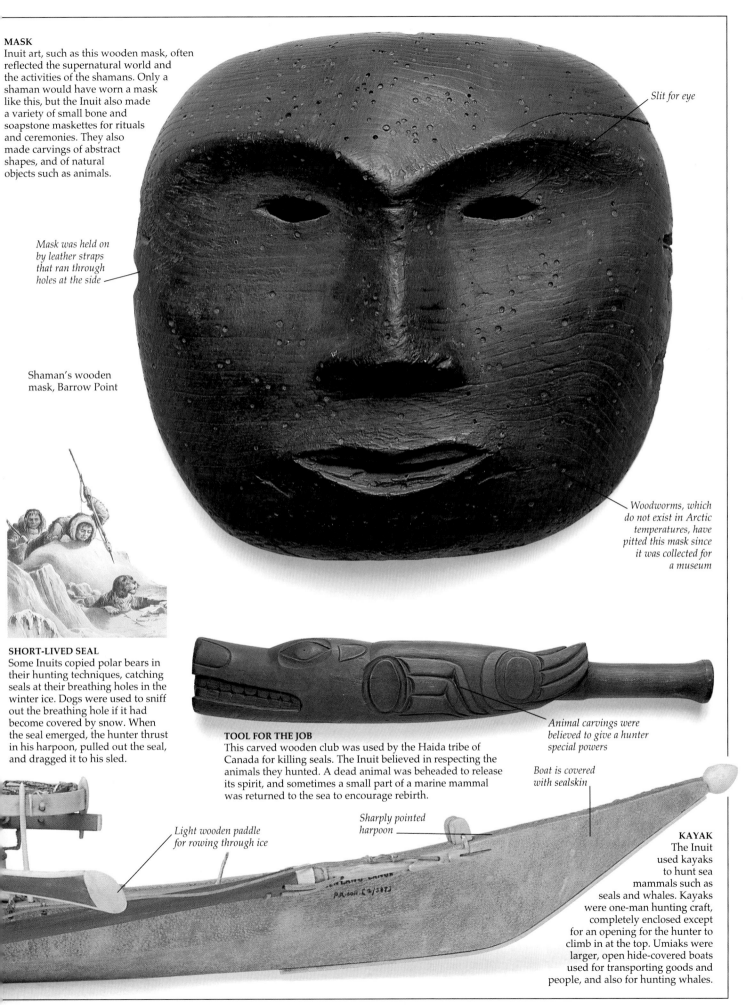

MASK
Inuit art, such as this wooden mask, often reflected the supernatural world and the activities of the shamans. Only a shaman would have worn a mask like this, but the Inuit also made a variety of small bone and soapstone maskettes for rituals and ceremonies. They also made carvings of abstract shapes, and of natural objects such as animals.

Slit for eye

Mask was held on by leather straps that ran through holes at the side

Shaman's wooden mask, Barrow Point

Woodworms, which do not exist in Arctic temperatures, have pitted this mask since it was collected for a museum

SHORT-LIVED SEAL
Some Inuits copied polar bears in their hunting techniques, catching seals at their breathing holes in the winter ice. Dogs were used to sniff out the breathing hole if it had become covered by snow. When the seal emerged, the hunter thrust in his harpoon, pulled out the seal, and dragged it to his sled.

TOOL FOR THE JOB
This carved wooden club was used by the Haida tribe of Canada for killing seals. The Inuit believed in respecting the animals they hunted. A dead animal was beheaded to release its spirit, and sometimes a small part of a marine mammal was returned to the sea to encourage rebirth.

Animal carvings were believed to give a hunter special powers

Boat is covered with sealskin

Light wooden paddle for rowing through ice

Sharply pointed harpoon

KAYAK
The Inuit used kayaks to hunt sea mammals such as seals and whales. Kayaks were one-man hunting craft, completely enclosed except for an opening for the hunter to climb in at the top. Umiaks were larger, open hide-covered boats used for transporting goods and people, and also for hunting whales.

Discovering the Arctic

Norwegian flag

IN THE 15TH CENTURY, European powers, intent on trade expansion, sponsored voyages into uncharted waters. Much early European exploration was centered on the search for a northern sea route to China and India, which would halve the time and danger involved in traveling overland. After the discovery of America, two routes were envisioned: the Northwest Passage, following the American coast, and the Northeast Passage, along the Siberian coast. The search for the Northwest Passage was soon monopolized by the British and the French but was later joined by the Americans; the Dutch and the Russians concentrated on the northeast. Over the next 350 years explorers opened up the Arctic, but it was not until 1878 that a Swede, Adolf Nordenskjïld, navigated the Northeast Passage, and 1905 when the great Norwegian explorer Roald Amundsen sailed through the Northwest Passage.

UP AND AWAY
Salomon Andrée, a Swedish aeronaut, and two companions tried to reach the North Pole in the balloon *Örnen* (*Eagle*) in 1897. The balloon was weighed down by ice and forced to land. All three men perished.

Sir John Franklin 1786–1847

Fox collar

RESCUE FOXES
Eight foxes were released in the Canadian Arctic wearing collars bearing the name and position of a rescue ship, and medals were distributed among the local people. It was hoped they might encounter Franklin survivors.

Medal

THE SEARCHERS
In 1845 Sir John Franklin led 128 men on a search for the Northwest Passage. By 1847 nothing had been heard from them, and his wife mobilized many expeditions to hunt for them. In fact, they had all died, but the searches greatly advanced geographical knowledge of the Arctic.

THE HOMECOMING
In 1818 John Ross (leading the procession), returned home to England, having failed to find the Northwest Passage but having succeeded in killing a bear! This cartoon was by George Cruickshank.

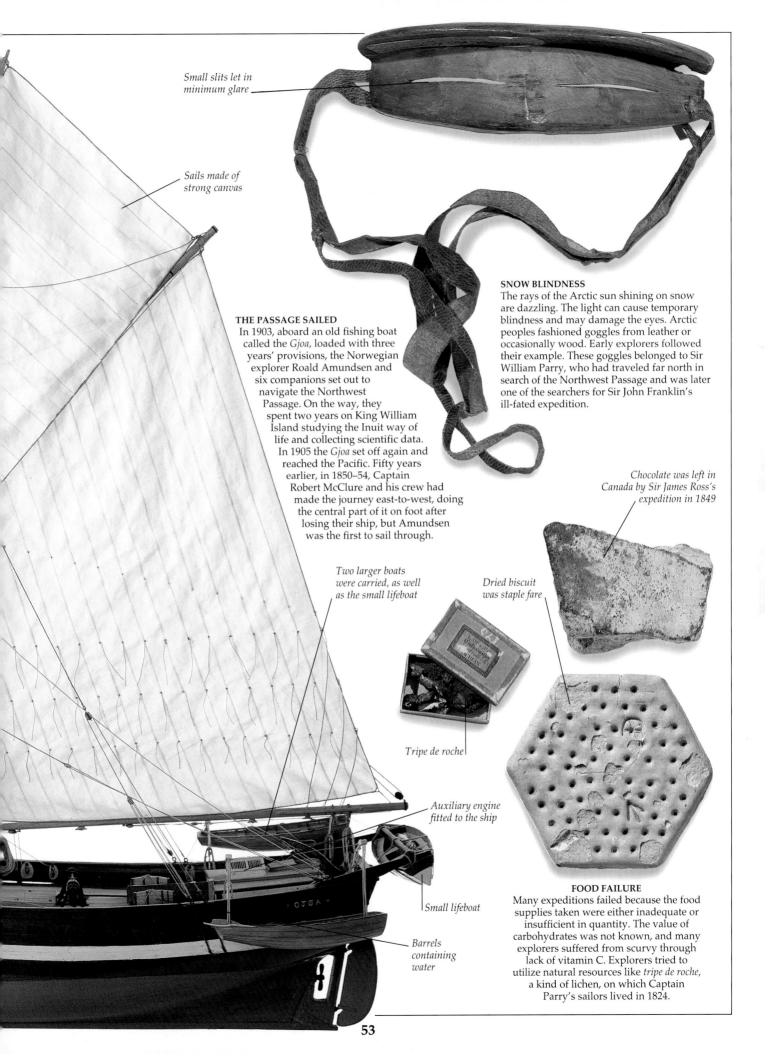

Small slits let in
minimum glare

Sails made of
strong canvas

SNOW BLINDNESS

The rays of the Arctic sun shining on snow
are dazzling. The light can cause temporary
blindness and may damage the eyes. Arctic
peoples fashioned goggles from leather or
occasionally wood. Early explorers followed
their example. These goggles belonged to Sir
William Parry, who had traveled far north in
search of the Northwest Passage and was later
one of the searchers for Sir John Franklin's
ill-fated expedition.

THE PASSAGE SAILED

In 1903, aboard an old fishing boat
called the *Gjoa*, loaded with three
years' provisions, the Norwegian
explorer Roald Amundsen and
six companions set out to
navigate the Northwest
Passage. On the way, they
spent two years on King William
Island studying the Inuit way of
life and collecting scientific data.
In 1905 the *Gjoa* set off again and
reached the Pacific. Fifty years
earlier, in 1850–54, Captain
Robert McClure and his crew had
made the journey east-to-west, doing
the central part of it on foot after
losing their ship, but Amundsen
was the first to sail through.

Chocolate was left in
Canada by Sir James Ross's
expedition in 1849

Two larger boats
were carried, as well
as the small lifeboat

Dried biscuit
was staple fare

Tripe de roche

Auxiliary engine
fitted to the ship

Small lifeboat

Barrels
containing
water

FOOD FAILURE

Many expeditions failed because the food
supplies taken were either inadequate or
insufficient in quantity. The value of
carbohydrates was not known, and many
explorers suffered from scurvy through
lack of vitamin C. Explorers tried to
utilize natural resources like *tripe de roche*,
a kind of lichen, on which Captain
Parry's sailors lived in 1824.

Scott and the Antarctic

Surveying the land

AT THE BEGINNING of the 20th century, several nations wanted to explore the Antarctic. In 1910, Robert Scott (1868–1912) from Britain set out for the South Pole. His expedition also had scientific objectives. After first using motorised sleds, ponies and dogs, and then hauling their own sleds through the harsh terrain, Scott and four companions, Wilson, Bowers, Oates, and Evans, finally arrived at the pole only to find that Norwegian explorer Roald Amundsen had reached it weeks before them. On the return journey the weather worsened, and weakened by cold and hunger, all five men perished. But although they lost the polar race, their scientific studies greatly advanced Antarctic science.

RUNNING REPAIRS
Dr. Wilson took this sewing kit on the ill-fated 1910–12 expedition. Keeping cotton and canvas clothing in good repair was essential in the harsh and difficult conditions.

Microscope magnifies the image inside the instrument

Günther & Tegetmeyer BRAUNSCHWEIG, No 4716.

Compact and lightweight kit for traveling

Side mirror reflects light into the instrument

BASE CAMP
From this desk in his "den" in base camp at Cape Evans, Scott wrote letters, reports, and his diary, studied maps, and planned the details of his trek to the pole. The extreme cold and the dry atmosphere have preserved the hut virtually as it was in 1910.

ELECTRIC SPIDER
This electrometer, taken by Scott to Antarctica, was used to measure tiny fluctuations in atmospheric electricity. If there was a difference in electric charge between the earth and the atmosphere, a small suspended mirror inside the electrometer would move. This movement was compared against the fixed line of a suspended fine filament from a black widow spider's web.

Wire to ground the instrument

String attached compass to a steady point

SUN ROUTE
This compass was used on Scott's 1910 expedition. From the time on a watch and the known position of the sun in the sky at that time, explorers could figure out a north-south direction using the compass and a chronometer.

POCKET HOSPITAL
A tiny medical kit was an essential part of polar expeditions. Injuries and frostbite had to be treated quickly in the harsh conditions.

Tablets of painkillers such as morphine and cocaine

Poisons such as strychnine were used for medicinal purposes

Syringe for administering standard doses of medicine

NEW LIFE
The *Terra Nova*, the ship in which Scott sailed to Antarctica on his last expedition, was originally a Scottish whaling vessel. Scott sailed to Cape Evans on Ross Island and set up his base camp there.

Instrument made mostly of brass so not affected by magnetic fields

LAST BASE
This pile of rocks marks the spot where the bodies of Scott, Wilson, and Bowers are buried. Only 11 miles (18 km) from a food depot, they were exhausted from hauling supplies and over 35 lb (15 kg) of geological specimens.

First to the pole

The Norwegian explorer Roald Amundsen (1872–1928) chose a different route to the pole than Scott. He also started his journey closer to the pole than Scott, setting up base camp at Framheim on the Ross Ice Shelf. Amundsen's expedition was better prepared and organized for fast travel than Scott's. They also took along more food. His polar party consisted of expert skiers and navigators and relied heavily on their dogs for transportation, and later, as food.

FLYING THE FLAG
Amundsen set out for the South Pole on October 20, 1911, across the previously unexplored Axel Heiberg glacier. He reached the pole on December 14, beating Scott by just over a month. Amundsen also made several expeditions to the Arctic, flying over the North Pole in the airship *Norge* in 1926. He was lost in a rescue mission in the Arctic in 1928.

ANTARCTICA

South Pole

Transantarctic Mountains

Ross Ice Shelf

Amundsen's route

Scott's route

Scott's last camp
Cape Evans

Framheim

Ross Sea

Keeping warm and safe

EARLY EXPLORERS SUFFERED greatly because they did not know how to keep warm and, equally important, dry, in harsh conditions. The freezing power of the icy winds was also largely ignored. Frostbite was very common and many men died of exposure. In time, lessons were learned from the native peoples, and by the early years of this century, equipment had improved enormously. Explorers used sleeping bags and fur boots and wore canvas jackets to protect themselves from the icy winds. Bringing the right food supplies was extremely important. On many early expeditions, too much emphasis was placed on the need for meat, and carbohydrates, vital for energy, were largely ignored. Today a great deal is known about the foods necessary for a healthy diet.

LAYER BY LAYER
The inadequacy of the clothes they wore contributed to the deaths of Captain Scott and his companions. They sweated a lot; the sweat froze, making the body cold and the clothes heavy and uncomfortable. Layers of lightweight clothes would have allowed good ventilation with the trapped air insulating against the cold.

Potato

Bolognaise sauce   Shepherd's pie

Cooking vessel

Polypropylene fabric takes moisture away from the body, preventing heat loss caused by sweat evaporation

Inner layer: "long johns" worn next to the skin

TRAVELING LIGHT
Traveling in the freezing polar landscapes is hard work, whether on skis or by snowmobile or sled. Therefore, food has to be light and compact and quick and easy to prepare. Dried foods that only have to be mixed with heated ice or snow fulfill all the requirements and are also nutritious.

Removable inner sole

FEET FIRST
The feet and the hands are particularly vulnerable to frostbite, so it is essential that these parts of the body are adequately covered. Today, different types of footwear have been designed for different conditions.

Thermal lining can be removed for easy drying

Padded sole for extra toughness

Adjustable lacing ensures a good fit

Glacier boots for use in deep powder snow

Thick, ridged rubber soles help prevent slipping

EYE SHADES
Goggles are worn to protect eyes from windblown snow and the glare of sunlight reflected off snow and ice.

Middle layer: fiberpile undergarment traps a layer of air, which is warmed by the body

ICE CRACKER
When climbing steep ice, two ice axes are hammered into the ice face. The climber then uses them to pull himself up.

Zippers allow garments to be easily removed

Waterproof nylon covering keeps the goosedown from becoming wet and losing insulating efficiency

Outer layer: jacket

Adjustable wrists prevent snow from entering mitt

For delicate outside work, thermal inner mitts are worn alone

Waterproof outer mitts are lined with fiberpile fabric for warmth

POLAR MAN
One of the many advantages of layer dressing is that the number of layers can be adjusted according to the activity of the wearer and the temperature. This outer layer, consisting of jacket and trousers, is filled with pure high-quality goosedown, which is the most efficient of natural fillings. Combined with the mid- and base layers, these garments provide insulation sufficient to keep warm at -40° F (-40° C).

Outer layer: high, padded trousers

Crampons attached to the soles provide grip

FOOT SUPPORT
These climbing boots are made of strong and fairly stiff plastic that supports the foot and ankle. They have a removable thermal lining.

Thermal socks worn next to the skin

Padded socks add extra warmth and help keep the feet dry

57

Polar travel

THE SNOW AND ICE of polar regions have always posed special problems for travelers. Snowshoes and skis keep people from sinking too far into soft snow, and boots with rough or spiked soles grip icy ground. Long, low sleds on smooth runners reduce friction and make it easier to move heavy loads over slippery, frozen surfaces. Early polar explorers learned from native Arctic peoples the benefits of using husky dogs to pull sleds. (Nomadic Lapp people used reindeer for the same purpose.) Modern motorized vehicles, such as the snowcat, with clawlike grips, or the snowmobile, with skis underneath, were developed from tried and tested traditional forms of transportation.

THE FIRST SNOWMOBILE
Scott's motorized sled was the first vehicle with caterpillar tracks to be designed especially for snow. The slats on the tracks helped to grip the snow. The vehicle was far ahead of its time, but it had an unreliable early gasoline engine and soon developed serious mechanical faults in the severe Antarctic environment. But it was a forerunner of the snowmobiles of today.

POLAR HORSESHOE
The pressure of a horse's or pony's hooves drives straight down through the snow, causing them to sink up to their bellies. The hooves also break through sea ice and snow bridges very easily. Snowshoes for horses and ponies help to spread out the weight so they have more chance of staying on the surface.

"Tennis racket" shape to spread weight as evenly as possible

A BRAVE MAN'S SHOES
These snowshoes were worn by Captain Oates, who perished on Scott's 1910–12 expedition to Antarctica. Oates's feet became frostbitten on the return journey, and then gangrenous. Rather than hold his companions up, he walked out of Scott's tent in a blizzard to die, so that they would be free to press on as fast as possible. His last words were "I am just going outside and may be some time." He hoped that this would enable his companions to save themselves, but tragically, his heroic gesture did not have the result he desired.

TOBOGGAN RUN
Sleds used in the Arctic and Antarctic need to be strong enough to carry heavy loads, but light enough for dogs or people to pull. Different types of sled suit different conditions. Narrow runners are best for hard ice, wide runners for soft snow. This wooden sled dates from 1934–37 and is loaded with scientific equipment, food, and medical supplies. A team of 12 huskies can pull a fully loaded sled weighing half a ton.

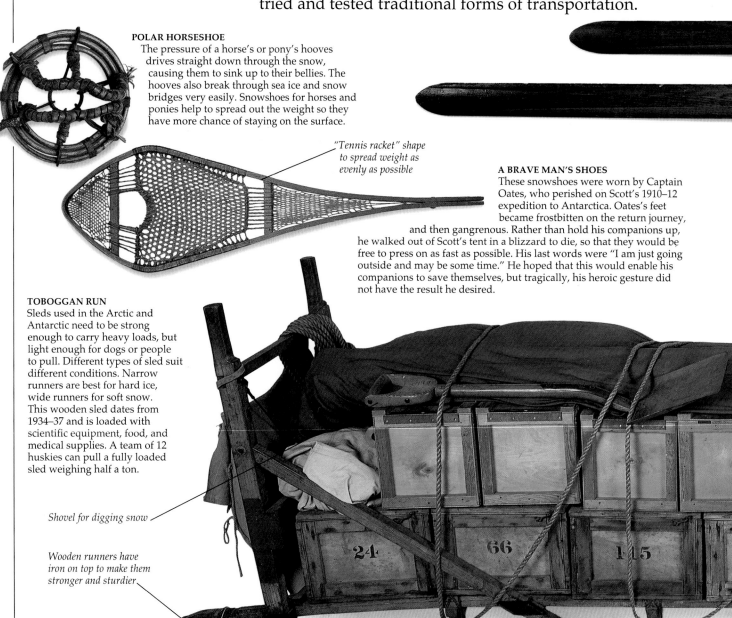

Shovel for digging snow

Wooden runners have iron on top to make them stronger and sturdier

Flat-bottomed sled like a toboggan "floats" easily over the surface of the snow without sinking in too far

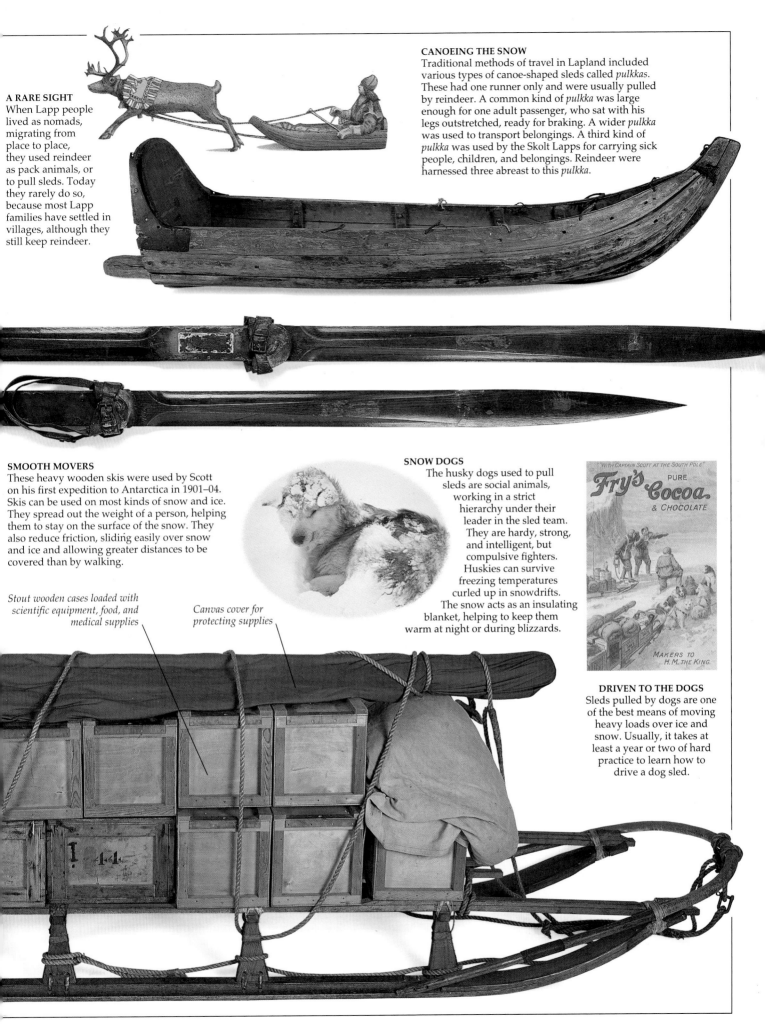

A RARE SIGHT
When Lapp people lived as nomads, migrating from place to place, they used reindeer as pack animals, or to pull sleds. Today they rarely do so, because most Lapp families have settled in villages, although they still keep reindeer.

CANOEING THE SNOW
Traditional methods of travel in Lapland included various types of canoe-shaped sleds called *pulkkas*. These had one runner only and were usually pulled by reindeer. A common kind of *pulkka* was large enough for one adult passenger, who sat with his legs outstretched, ready for braking. A wider *pulkka* was used to transport belongings. A third kind of *pulkka* was used by the Skolt Lapps for carrying sick people, children, and belongings. Reindeer were harnessed three abreast to this *pulkka*.

SMOOTH MOVERS
These heavy wooden skis were used by Scott on his first expedition to Antarctica in 1901–04. Skis can be used on most kinds of snow and ice. They spread out the weight of a person, helping them to stay on the surface of the snow. They also reduce friction, sliding easily over snow and ice and allowing greater distances to be covered than by walking.

SNOW DOGS
The husky dogs used to pull sleds are social animals, working in a strict hierarchy under their leader in the sled team. They are hardy, strong, and intelligent, but compulsive fighters. Huskies can survive freezing temperatures curled up in snowdrifts. The snow acts as an insulating blanket, helping to keep them warm at night or during blizzards.

Stout wooden cases loaded with scientific equipment, food, and medical supplies

Canvas cover for protecting supplies

"WITH CAPTAIN SCOTT AT THE SOUTH POLE"
Fry's PURE Cocoa & CHOCOLATE
MAKERS TO H. M. THE KING.

DRIVEN TO THE DOGS
Sleds pulled by dogs are one of the best means of moving heavy loads over ice and snow. Usually, it takes at least a year or two of hard practice to learn how to drive a dog sled.

59

Life at the poles

The CRUEL SEAS, savage and unpredictable climates, and inhospitable terrains of the two polar regions have ensured that neither environment has ever been completely conquered by humans. The history of polar exploration is one of appalling hardship and terrible toll of human life. However, in the Arctic, the Inuit peoples evolved survival skills over the centuries that enabled them to live a fruitful existence. European explorers learned much from their way of life and gradually applied this knowledge to their own ability to explore and live in these harsh environments. Today, the lifestyle at the poles for both Inuits and other polar dwellers is very similar. Scientific advances in clothing, transportation, food, and building have ensured a way of life far removed from the hardships of earlier times.

HELPING HANDS
Many early explorers died because they could not build strong enough shelters. By the 19th century, Arctic explorers realized how much they could learn from the native peoples.

EFFICIENT RECYCLING
On Scott's last expedition, Edward Wilson made a successful candlestick out of a cracker box. Explorers tried to find an alternative use for everything.

Window made from a block of freshwater ice

Entrance passage   *Storage alcove*

OVERNIGHT STAY
Today, some Inuits still build igloos as temporary shelter. Here the hunter is lighting his primus stove, with which he will warm himself and cook his dinner.

SNOW HOUSE
Contrary to popular belief, Inuits never built igloos as permanent homes, but as temporary bases during the winter seal-hunting season. For much of the time they lived partly underground in dwellings made on a frame of driftwood or whalebone and covered by grass.

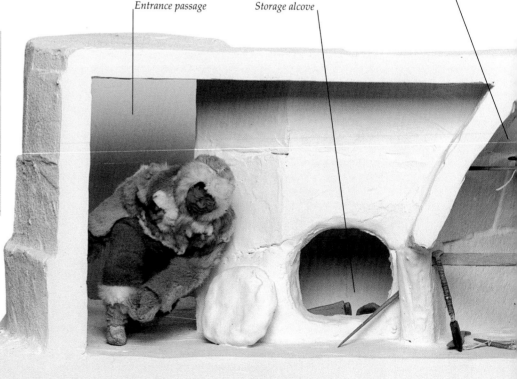

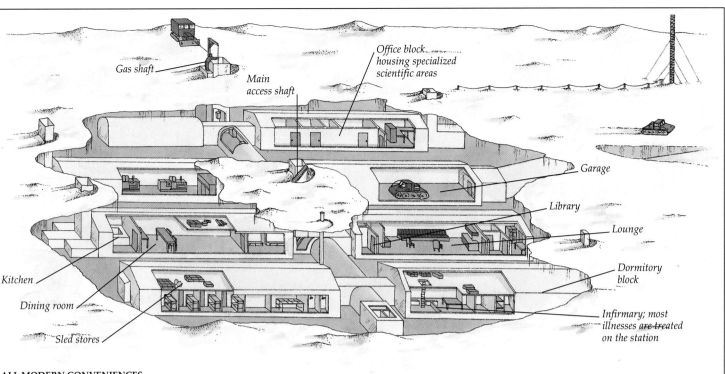

Gas shaft

Main access shaft

Office block housing specialized scientific areas

Garage

Library

Lounge

Dormitory block

Infirmary; most illnesses are treated on the station

Kitchen

Dining room

Sled stores

ALL MODERN CONVENIENCES
Today several countries have large research stations in the Antarctic, some permanent and some temporary. Most stations are involved in scientific surveys in geology, geophysics, glaciology, terrestrial biology, and atmospheric sciences. Several stations, like Britain's Halley Station, have been built underground. Halley has been built four times, as each of the successive structures has been crushed by the steadily shifting ice sheet.

SKIDDING AROUND
Polar travel is no longer reliant on dogs or ponies. Today most people travel on snowmobiles, which are small motorized sleds on skis. They are easy to maneuver and pull very heavy loads.

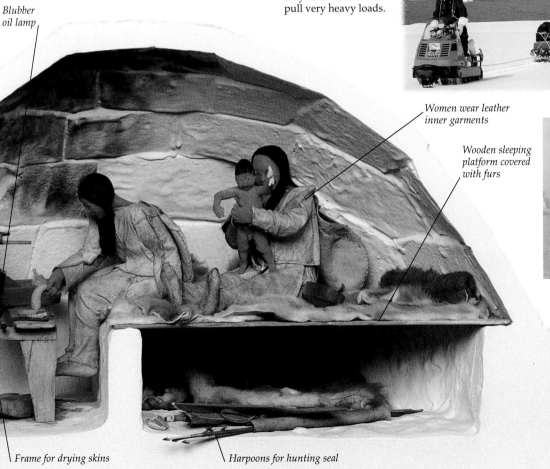

Blubber oil lamp

Women wear leather inner garments

Wooden sleeping platform covered with furs

Frame for drying skins

Harpoons for hunting seal

LAB OF THE NORTH
Canada has several research laboratories in the Arctic. This space-age laboratory at Igloolik in Canada's Northwest Territories has contributed much to scientific knowledge of the Arctic region.

Domino-shaped blocks of frozen snow

Last frontiers

GARBAGE DISPOSAL
The way people dispose of their trash in the Arctic and Antarctic often pollutes or damages the environment. Garbage dumps on the edge of Churchill, Canada, attract polar bears, which can be poisoned or injured by eating the garbage. The bears' nearness also causes fears for people's safety.

AT THE HEIGHT OF SUMMER in the Antarctic, tourist ships move gently around the coast. Even 30 years ago such sights would have been unthinkable, but today people are willing to pay large sums of money to see the last real wilderness in the world. In the Arctic, careless human exploitation in the past has damaged the fragile ecosystem. Today concerned governments are trying to find ways to develop the region while caring for the very special natural environment. Because the Antarctic is less accessible than the Arctic, it is still largely undamaged by humans, although holes in the ozone layer above the Antarctic have already been discovered. Many people believe that one way to preserve the area is to make the whole region into a world park, with every form of exploitation internationally banned. It is important to conserve the Arctic and Antarctic so that future generations can experience these extraordinary environments with their unique wildlife in their natural state.

DAY TRIPPERS
Tourist visits to the Antarctic have to be carefully monitored and organized, as tourists could damage fragile vegetation and disturb nesting and breeding grounds. On the other hand, tourist visits can help to spread concern for conservation.

All snowflakes have six points

LANDS OF SNOW
The permanence of snow and ice in the Arctic and Antarctic is what makes these regions unique. Snow reflects the sun's rays, helping to keep temperatures low at all times.

Crystals growing in random directions

Lines of striations formed as the crystal grew

Well-developed crystal faces

Copper on limonite

Dendritic copper

Rock crystal

Limonite groundmass

MINING PRESSURE
The Arctic is mined for oil, coal, and other minerals. Roads, mines, ports, pipelines, and airstrips disturb wildlife and damage the fragile ecosystem. Several minerals have already been found in the Antarctic, but the costs of exploiting them, together with increasing pressure to protect the environment, have led the Antarctic Treaty nations to agree to ban mining until 2041.

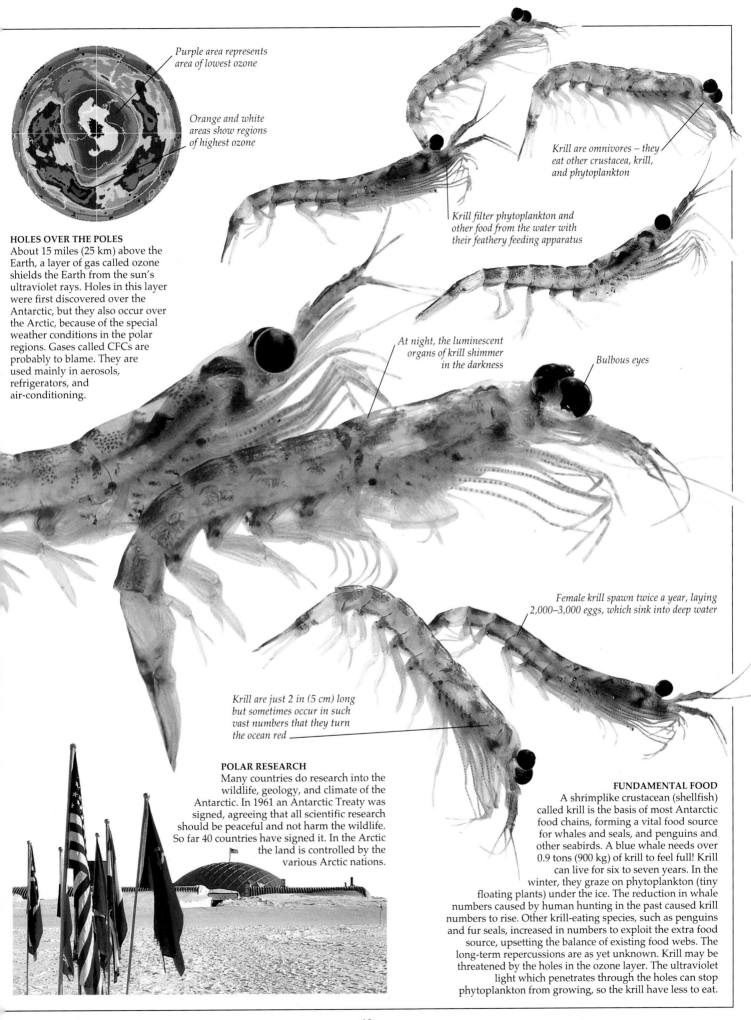

HOLES OVER THE POLES

About 15 miles (25 km) above the Earth, a layer of gas called ozone shields the Earth from the sun's ultraviolet rays. Holes in this layer were first discovered over the Antarctic, but they also occur over the Arctic, because of the special weather conditions in the polar regions. Gases called CFCs are probably to blame. They are used mainly in aerosols, refrigerators, and air-conditioning.

Purple area represents area of lowest ozone

Orange and white areas show regions of highest ozone

Krill are omnivores – they eat other crustacea, krill, and phytoplankton

Krill filter phytoplankton and other food from the water with their feathery feeding apparatus

At night, the luminescent organs of krill shimmer in the darkness

Bulbous eyes

Female krill spawn twice a year, laying 2,000–3,000 eggs, which sink into deep water

Krill are just 2 in (5 cm) long but sometimes occur in such vast numbers that they turn the ocean red

POLAR RESEARCH

Many countries do research into the wildlife, geology, and climate of the Antarctic. In 1961 an Antarctic Treaty was signed, agreeing that all scientific research should be peaceful and not harm the wildlife. So far 40 countries have signed it. In the Arctic the land is controlled by the various Arctic nations.

FUNDAMENTAL FOOD

A shrimplike crustacean (shellfish) called krill is the basis of most Antarctic food chains, forming a vital food source for whales and seals, and penguins and other seabirds. A blue whale needs over 0.9 tons (900 kg) of krill to feel full! Krill can live for six to seven years. In the winter, they graze on phytoplankton (tiny floating plants) under the ice. The reduction in whale numbers caused by human hunting in the past caused krill numbers to rise. Other krill-eating species, such as penguins and fur seals, increased in numbers to exploit the extra food source, upsetting the balance of existing food webs. The long-term repercussions are as yet unknown. Krill may be threatened by the holes in the ozone layer. The ultraviolet light which penetrates through the holes can stop phytoplankton from growing, so the krill have less to eat.

Index

Acknowledgments

Dorling Kindersley would like to thank:
Open Air Cambridge Ltd. for the use of their clothing and equipment; the staff of Tierpark Dählhölzli, Bern, Switzerland, for their time and trouble; Tony Hall at the Royal Botanical Gardens, Kew; Julia Nicholson and the Pitt Rivers Museum, Oxford; Robert Headland and the staff of the Scott Polar Institute, Cambridge; Whipsnade Zoo, Bedfordshire; The British School of Falconry, Gleneagles, Scotland; Ivan Finnegan, Kati Poynor, Robin Hunter, Manisha Patel, Andrew Nash, Susan St.Louis, and Aude van Ryn for design and illustration assistance.

Additional photography: Lynton Gardiner at the American Museum of Natural History (60/61b); Neil Fletcher (1c); Dave King (37cr); Minden Pictures

(42cl); Harry Taylor at the Natural History Museum (45tl, 47tr); University Museum, Cambridge (43cr); Jerry Young (16cl, 17c, 32/33, 40tl)
Index:
Hilary Bird
Maps:
Sallie Alane Reason
Model:
Gordon Models

Picture credits
t=top b=bottom c=centre l=left r=right

Aardman Animations: 28cr
Ardea: 36c; /Jean-Paul Ferrero 28bc; /François Gohier 45cr; /Graham Robertson 30c
B & C Alexander: 6/7b, 8bl, 11ctr, 15t, 21c, 23c, 25br, 38tl, 39ctr, 42bl, 42/43b, 44bl, 44br, 59c, 60cbl, 61cbr, 62tl, 62tr; /Paul Drummond 23tl; /NASA 63tl
Barnaby's Picture Library /Rothman: 6/7c

Bridgeman Art Library: 25tl; /British Library 7tl; /National Maritime Museum 52cl
British Antarctic Survey: 10tr, 12ctl, 23bl; /D.G. Allan 13 tr, 13br; /C.J. Gilbert 10cl, 10bl, 12tl; /E. Jarvis 45br ; /B. Thomas 61cr
Bruce Coleman Ltd: 14/15b, 34tl, 35bl, 36bl, 36br; Jen & Des Bartlett 20cl /Roger A. Goggan 12/13; /Johnny Johnson 7tr; /Stephen J. Krasemann 19br; /Len Rue Jr. 40bl; /John Shaw 41c; /Keith Nels Swenson 11ctl; /Rinie van Meurs 29cr
ET Archive: 6tr
Mary Evans Picture Library: 8tl, 9tr, 38tr, 40cr, 41tr, 42tl, 46tr, 54bl, 55ct, 55cr, 55bc, 56tl
Illustrated London News: 20tl, 26cr
Frank Lane Picture Agency: /Hannu Hautala 17tcl; /E&D Hosking 22c; /Peter Moore 14cl; /F. Pölking 32cl; /Mark Newman 38c; /Tony Wharton 17tl
Natural History Photographic Agency: /B&C Alexander 10/11; /Melvin Grey 20/21b; /Brian Hawkes 29tl; /Tony Howard /ANT 10c; /E.A. James 29tr;

/Peter Johnson 27c; /Stephen Krasemann 37tr; /Lady Philippa Scott 27bl
Robert Opie Collection: 59cr
Oxford Scientific Films: 27ctl; /Doug Allan 12c, 12b, 16bl, 30tl, 44ctr; /Michael Brooke 22tl; /S.R. Maglione 14/15t; /Colin Monteath 22b; /S.R. Morris 35cl; /Owen Newman 20ctl; /Ben Osborne 26bl, 28l, 29b; /Richard Packwood 36tl; /Konrad Wothe 32bcr
Planet Earth Pictures: /Gary Bell 33tcl; /Peter Scoones 29tc; /Scott McKinley 9cr; /Bora Merdsoy 13bl
Royal Geographical Society: 53cr, 53tr, 56cl; /Alastair Laidlaw 53br
Science Photo Library: /Dr. David Millar 63bl; /Claude Nuridsany & Marie Perennou 62cl
Zefa Picture Library: /Allstock 31c; /Frans Lanting 26tl

Every effort has been made to trace the copyright holders. Dorling Kindersley apologises for any unintentional omissions and would be pleased, in such cases, to add an acknowledgment in future editions.